Chrisya R Caudle

Growing with Music

HARRY R. WILSON

WALTER EHRET

ALICE M. SNYDER

EDWARD J. HERMANN

ALBERT A. RENNA

Illustrated by JOHN MOODIE

BOOK 7

Prentice-Hall, Inc.

Englewood Cliffs, New Jersey

The authors of *Growing with Music* wish to thank the many people who have contributed original material for this book. Every effort has been made to locate owners of other materials and grateful acknowledgment is due these publishers for permission to reprint copyrighted materials.

HARRY R. WILSON, Chairman of the Music Department
Teachers College, Columbia University

WALTER EHRET, Supervisor of Vocal Music
Scarsdale Schools, Scarsdale, New York

ALICE M. SNYDER, Professor of Music Education
San Francisco State College

EDWARD J. HERMANN, Associate Professor of Music
Louisiana State University

ALBERT A. RENNA, Director of Music
San Francisco Unified School District

As an aid to teaching and interpretation, all songs in "Growing with Music,"
Book 7, are recorded and are available in a boxed set
of 12-inch L.P. records, from Prentice-Hall, Inc.

The music in this book was reproduced from handwritten originals by Maxwell Weaner.

©1966 by PRENTICE-HALL, INC., Englewood Cliffs, N.J.

Printed in the United States of America

36603—E

2 3 4 5 6 7 8 9 10

Contents

Should my way be dark and lonely,
Should the path be steep and long,
Put upon my lips a prayer
And into my heart a song.
        —M. A. DUFAY

Mood in Music

The Home Road

WORDS AND MUSIC
BY JOHN ALDEN CARPENTER

Moderato

f 1. Sing a hymn of free - dom, Hold the ban - ner high!
p 2. In the qui - et hours ____ of the star - ry night,

Sing the songs of lib - er - ty, Songs that shall not die.
Dream - ing dreams of far a - way, Plac - es far from sight.

mf For the long, long road that goes a - wind - ing, Is the road that

leads me home, ____ *f* O'er hills and plains, by lakes and lanes;

My wood - lands, my wheat - fields, my coun - try, my home.

The Erlking

WORDS BY GOETHE
MUSIC BY FRANZ SCHUBERT

"The Erlking" is written for one solo voice, but the singer must represent four different characters — narrator, father, child, and Erlking. Because the song is a miniature drama, the English translation on the opposite page has been printed like the script of a play, with the characters clearly marked. Read the translation and after you are familiar with the story, listen for the different moods in the recording.

The piano begins the song with a musical picture of the wild, stormy night and the galloping horse.

In quick succession we hear the narrator, the father, and the child. Notice that when the Erlking speaks, the accompaniment figure changes to this pattern.

When he is finished, the piano returns to the music of the first example. Later in the song, the Erlking again tempts the boy but to a still different accompaniment.

In his final speech, the Erlking's accompaniment is the first example, almost as though he had caught up with the riders and was galloping at their side. Listen for the dramatic chords in the last line and the pause before the words, "was dead."

Wer reitet so spät durch Nacht und Wind?
Es ist der Vater mit seinem Kind;
Er hat den Knaben wohl in dem Arm,
Er fasst ihn sicher, er hält ihn warm.

Mein Sohn, was birgst du so bang dein Gesicht?

Siehst, Vater, du den Erlkönig nicht?
Den Erlenkönig mit Kron' und Schweif?

Mein Sohn, es ist ein Nebelstreif.

"Du liebes Kind, komm, geh' mit mir!
Gar schöne Spiele spiel' ich mit dir;
Manch' bunte Blumen sind an dem Strand,
Meine Mutter hat manch gülden Gewand."

Mein Vater, mein Vater, und hörest du nicht,
Was Erlenkönig mir leise verspricht?

Sei ruhig, bleibe ruhig, mein Kind;
In dürren Blättern säuselt der Wind.

"Willst, feiner Knabe, du mit mir geh'n?
Meine Töchter sollen dich warten schön
Meine Töchter führen den nächtlichen Reih'n
Und wiegen und tanzen und singen dich ein,
Sie wiegen und tanzen und singen dich ein."

Mein Vater, mein Vater, und siehst du nicht dort
Erlkönigs Töchter am düstern Ort?

Mein Sohn, mein Sohn, ich seh' es genau,
Es scheinen die alten Weiden so grau.

"Ich liebe dich, mich reizt deine schöne Gestalt,
Und bist du nicht willig, so brauch' ich Gewalt."

Mein Vater, mein Vater, jetzt fasst er mich an!
Erlkönig hat mir ein Leid's gethan!

Dem Vater grauset's, er reitet geschwind,
Er hält in Armen das ächzenden Kind,
Erreicht den Hof mit Müh und Noth;
In seinem Armen das Kind war todt.

NARRATOR:
Who rides so late in night and wind?
It is a father and his son.
He has the boy in his arms
And holds him tightly to keep him warm.

FATHER:
"My son, why make such an anxious face?"

SON:
"Oh, father, don't you see the Erlking?
The Erlking with crown and robe."

FATHER:
"My son, it's only a wisp of fog."

ERLKING:
"You lovely child, come, go with me,
Such happy games I'll play with you.
Many radiant flowers bloom near my house,
My mother has golden clothes for you."

SON:
"Oh, father, father, do you hear
What the Erlking softly promises me?"

FATHER:
"Be still, be still, my child,
It's only the wind rattling the dead leaves."

ERLKING:
"Will you go with me, you wonderful boy?
My daughters will wait on you,
And every night they'll dance with you,
They'll sing and dance and lull you to sleep
They'll sing and dance and lull you to sleep."

SON:
"Father, father, you surely must see
Erlking's daughters waiting for me."

FATHER:
"My son, my son, of course I see;
The waving branches of an old willow tree."

ERLKING:
"You've got to come, you handsome boy,
And if not freely, I'll take you by force!"

SON:
"Father, father, he's caught hold of me!
Erlking is crushing me so!"

NARRATOR:
The father shudders and gallops his horse.
He holds his moaning child in his arms,
Arrives at the courtyard with fear and dread,
And in his arms, the child...was dead.

The Pearl

WORDS BY MARTA HARO
SPANISH FOLK MELODY

Some of the phrases in this song move in strict
dotted rhythm patterns, while others move freely
in triplets and smooth-flowing sixteenth notes.
What does this contrast contribute to the mood?

'Neath the deep sea, a love-ly pearl was ly-ing. High on a hill top,
En el fon-do del mar na-ció la per-la, En la al-ta ro-ca

pur-ple flow-ers grew. In the white clouds, the dew was bright-ly shin-ing,
la vio-le-ta a a-zul; En-tre nu-bes la go-ta de ro-cí-o

And I lay dream-ing, dream-ing of none but you. The pearl has van-ished,
Y en mis en-sue-ños, y en mis en-sue-ños tú. Mu-rió la per-la

sent to a dis-tant is-land. And now in mar-ble urns the flow-ers die.
en im-per-ial co-ro-na en bú-ca-ro gen-til la cas-ta flor,

In the dark clouds, the dew to mist is fad-ing.
En la no-che la go-ta de ro-cí-o,

And in my dream-ing, I hear you say good-by.
y en tu me-mo-ria, y en tu me-mo-ria yo.

Like many Spanish folk melodies, "La Perla" is harmonized at the interval of a third below the melody. Can
you find and name the intervals other than thirds used
in the harmony part? Does the mood of the song change
if the harmony part is hummed rather than sung?

4

Instruments can enhance the mood of a song
(see page 128). The violin is traditionally
associated with sad gypsy-like tunes and its
plaintive tones add a wistful countermelody.

Dark Eyes

WORDS BY ROBERT REYNOLDS
RUSSIAN FOLK MELODY

Dark eyes haunt-ing me ____ Like a mel-o-dy. ____ Ev-er
Eyes with spark-ling fire ____ Fill'd me with de-sire. ____ Will I

tell-ing me ____ Of what used to be. ____ How they
al-ways dwell ____ 'Neath their mag-ic spell? ____ Ev-'ry-

tan-ta-lize, ____ Those en-chant-ing eyes, ____ Now they sing to me ____
where I see ____ Their deep mys-ter-y, ____ They keep haunt-ing me ____

1.
____ in a min-or key.

2.
____ like a mem-o-ry.

5

Everything's Fine!

TRANS. BY M. A. DUFAY
MUSIC BY PAUL MISRAKI

Moderately

mf

1. Hel - lo, hel - lo, James, what is the news there?
2. Hel - lo, hel - lo, James, what are you say - ing?

I've called to know what's go - ing on.
My chest - nut mare was killed to - day?

It's been a - while, and I've been else - where,
Now tell me, James, with - out de - lay - ing,

Fine

How's ev - 'ry - thing since I've been gone?
What's go - ing on while I'm a - way?

Ev - 'ry - thing's fine, Ma - da - me la Mar - qui - se,
Ev - 'ry - thing's fine, Ma - da - me la Mar - qui - se,

Ev - 'ry - thing's fine, Things are just fine.
Ev - 'ry - thing's fine, Things are just fine.

But I must say, there is a lit - tle some - thing,
But I must say, since you have so in - quir - ed,

It hap-pened while you were a-way.
(Hys-ter-ics I would not pro-voke!)

Yes, I must say, a rath-er trou-ble-some thing,
But at the time your chest-nut mare ex-pir-ed,

Your chest-nut mare was killed to-day.
Your sta-ble, too, went up in smoke.

Oth-er than that, Ma-da-me la Mar-qui-se,
Oth-er than that, Ma-da-me la Mar-qui-se,

Ev-'ry-thing's fine, Things are just fine! ___
Ev-'ry-thing's fine, Things are just fine! ___

3. Hello, hello, James, this is amazing,
   My horse and stable are no more.
   And the Marquis, while things were blazing,
   Did he go through the nearest door?

   Well, sad to say, Madame la Marquise,
   When the Marquis viewed the tableau,
   He shot himself, It's really not surprising,
   He shot himself quite dead, you know.

   And when he fell, he knocked the candles over,
   So that's the end of your chateau!
   Other than that, Madame la Marquise
   Ev'rything's fine, Things are just fine!

4. Hello, hello, James, it's quite unheard of,
   This shocking news I do bemoan,
   It's really odd, the things one learns of
   When calling on the telephone! (*Fine*)

If Thou be Near

TRANS. BY IVAN TRUSLER
MUSIC BY JOHANN SEBASTIAN BACH

A mood of serene faith, as expressed
in the words, is perfectly mirrored
in the calm, slow-moving accompaniment.

If thou be near, then I wait calm - ly to greet __ my __
Bist du bei mir, geh' ich mit Freu - den zum Ster - ben __

death with grate - ful __ heart, to _____ greet my death with grate - ful heart.
und zu mei - ner __ Ruh', zum _____ Ster - ben und zu mei - ner Ruh'!

If thou __ be __ near, then I wait calm - ly to greet __ my
Bist du __ bei __ mir, geh' ich mit Freu - den zum Ster - ben __

8

death with grate - ful _ heart, to _ greet my death with grate - ful heart.
und zu mei - ner _ Ruh', zum _ Ster - ben und zu mei - ner Ruh'!

mf O hap - py life, O per - fect end - ing, with thy _ blest _
Ach, wie ver - gnügt wär' so mein En - de, es drück - ten _

hand up - on _ my brow _ when at _ last my eye - lids close in death.
dei - ne lie - ben Hän - de mir _ die ge - treu - en Au - gen zu!

mf O hap - py life, O per - fect end - ing, with thy _ blest _
Ach, wie ver - gnügt wär' so mein En - de, es drück - ten _

hand up - on __ my __ brow __ when at __ last my eye - lids close in death.
dei - ne lie - ben Hän - de mir __ die ge - treu - en Au - gen zu!

If thou __ be __ near, then I wait calm - ly, to greet __ my __
Bist du __ bei __ mir, geh' ich mit Freu - den zum Ster - ben __

death with grate - ful __ heart, to _____ greet my death with grate - ful heart.
und zu mei - ner __ Ruh', zum _____ Ster - ben und zu mei - ner Ruh'!

This beautiful song is one of several that Bach wrote for his
wife, Anna Magdalena. It can be interpreted either as a love
song or as a declaration of deep religious faith. Because of
this double significance, it is frequently sung to enhance the
devotional mood at wedding ceremonies.

10

Water Come a' Me Eye

CARIBBEAN FOLK SONG

Sing this song very quickly, then
very slowly. The words and music are
the same, but how has the mood changed?

Rhythmically

1. Ev - 'ry - time I 'mem - ber Li - za, Wa - ter come __ a' me eye,
2. I still wait - in' home for Li - za, Wa - ter come __ a' me eye.

Ev - 'ry time I think 'pon Li - za, Wa - ter come __ a' me eye.
Heart is sore but wait - in', Li - za,

Come __ back, __ Li - - - za,

REFRAIN

Come back, Li - za, come back, gal, Wipe the tear __ from me eye,

Come __ back, __ Li - - - za.

Come back, Li - za, come back, gal, Wipe the tear __ from me eye.

The two patterns above may be used for strumming accompanying instruments such as guitar and ukulele. You
might also play these patterns on rhythm instruments
most often used in the Caribbean area (see page 128).

Will Ye No' Come Back Again?

WORDS BY LADY NAIRNE
MUSIC BY NEIL GOW

1. Bon - nie Char - lie's noo a - wa; Safe - ly owre the friend - ly main;
2. Ye trust - ed in your Hie - lan' men, They trust - ed you, dear Char - lie,

Mo - ny a heart will break in twa, Should he ne'er come back a - gain.
They kent your hid - ing in the glen, Death or ex - ile brav - ing.

REFRAIN

Will ye no' come back a - gain, Will ye no' come, back a - gain?

Bet- ter lo'ed ye can- na be, Will ye no' come back___ a- gain?

3. We watched thee in the gloamin' hour,
   We watched thee in the mornin' grey;
   Tho' thirty thousand pound they gie,
   Oh, there is nane that wad betray!

   REFRAIN

4. Sweet the laverock's note and lang,
   Liltin' wildly up the glen;
   But aye to me he sings ae sang,
   Will ye no come back again?

   REFRAIN

Get on Board

Both "Bist Du Bei Mir" (page 8) and "Get on Board"
express strong faith. How do they differ in mood?

SPIRITUAL

Get on board, ___ Get on board, ___ Get on board, ___ Get on board. ___

SOLO VOICE (OR SMALL GROUP)

1. The gos-pel train's a-com-in'. I hear it just at hand. ___ I
2. I hear the train a-com-in', a-com-in' round the curve. ___ She

(Hum) ___

hear the car wheels roll-in' ___ And rum-blin' through the land.
loos-ened all her steam and brakes, She's strain-in' ev-'ry nerve.

(Hum) ___

14

The up and down movement of this melody gives a swinging quality to the song. The upper harmony part adds an extra lilt when it moves in faster note values.

Summer Ends

WORDS BY YVONNE CARR
MUSIC BY EMANUEL R. HEIFETZ

1. Sum - mer ends ___ and so once ___ a - gain, ___ Say fare - well to friends ___
2. Win - ter goes, ___ as ev - 'ry - one knows, ___ And spring melts the snows ___

And sweet sum - mer weath - er. ___ Have no fear ___ tho' win - ter ___ is near, ___
Of cold win - ter weath - er. ___ Skies will clear ___ for sum - mer ___ is near, ___

Sing praise of the days we have spent ___ to - geth - er. ___
Sing praise of the days we will spend ___ to - geth - er. ___

Our Hearts Lift with Gladness

TRANS. BY GILBERT COOK
ISRAELI FOLK TUNE

What is the form of this melody?
Are the sections the same length?

Vigorously

S

Our hearts lift with glad - ness, Our hearts lift with glad - ness,
Ve - ta - her li - be - nu, ve - ta - her li - be - nu,

A

Our hearts with glad - ness, Our __ hearts with glad - ness
Ta - her li - be - nu, Ve - ta - her li - be - nu,

Our hearts lift with glad - ness, for truth shall ban - ish sad - ness.
Ve - ta - her li - be - nu, le - ov - de - cha be - e - met.

Hearts __ lift with glad - ness for truth shall ban - ish sad - ness.
Ve - ta - her li - be - nu, le - ov - de - cha be - e - met.

Re - joice, re - joice, re - joice, re - joice, re - joice!
Ta - her, ta - her, ta - her, ta - her, ta - her!

Re - joice, re - joice, re - joice! Re - joice
Ta - her, ta - her, ta - her, ta - her,

16

Doney Gal

OKLAHOMA FOLK SONG

What has the artist done in this picture to help intensify the mood?

Slowly

We're a - lone, Do - ney Gal, in the wind and hail, —
Got to drive these — do - gies — down the trail. —

1. We'll ride the range from sun to sun,
2. A cow - boy's life is a wea - ry thing,

For a cow - boy's work is — nev - er done;
For it's rope — and brand and — ride and sing;

He's up and gone at the break of day,
Yes, day or night, in the rain or hail, He'll

Driv - in' the do - gies on their wea - ry — way.
stay with his do - gies out — on the — trail.

3. Rain or shine, sleet or snow,
   Me and my Doney Gal are on the go;
   We travel down that lonesome trail
   Where a man and his horse seldom ever fail.

4. We whoop at the sun and yell through the hail,
   But we drive the poor dogies down the trail;
   And we'll laugh at the storms, the sleet and the snow,
   When we reach the little town of San Antonio.

18

Carmen Overture

FROM "CARMEN"
BY GEORGES BIZET

"Carmen" is a dramatic and emotional opera by Georges Bizet. As one might expect, the music is also highly emotional and conveys many different moods.

The opera is set in and near the Spanish city of Seville, around 1820. Carmen, a lovely gypsy girl, and Don José, a corporal of the guards, are attracted to each other and fall in love. To be with Carmen, Don José deserts from the army and joins a band of smugglers. In their camp, Carmen meets Escamillo, a *toreador*. By this time she is bored with Don José and leaves him in favor of Escamillo. In the last act of the opera, Don José confronts Carmen in the empty square before the bullring where Escamillo is fighting. He pleads with her to return to him but she tells him that all is over between them. As their argument becomes more and more violent, we hear the noise of the bullfight in the background. Just as the triumphant Escamillo and the crowd return from the bullfight, Don José stabs and kills Carmen.

The Overture to "Carmen" is made up of two main themes. First we hear the brilliant processional music that is played in the last act as Escamillo and his attendants enter the bullring.

Then we hear the famous "Song of the Toreador." What is the mood of the music? Does it fit the character of Escamillo? Following the "Song of the Toreador," we hear again the opening procession music. However, after the repetition of the first theme, Bizet tells us very clearly that Carmen will end tragically. The ominous music that ends the overture is known as the "Fate" theme and is the same music played at the end of the opera when Carmen is killed.

Three Doves

WORDS ADAPTED BY T. VELOTTA
ITALIAN FOLK SONG

By following the contour of the melody
with your hand, you can trace in the air
the graceful flight of the three doves.

1. Three doves are fly - ing, _____
2. The doves are go - ing, _____
3. The doves are soar - ing, _____

1. In the sky, _____ three doves _____ are fly - ing, _____ In the
2. O'er the sea, _____ the doves _____ are go - ing, _____ O'er the
3. On white wings, _____ the doves _____ are soar - ing, _____ On white

Three doves are fly - ing, __ Three doves are
The doves are go - ing, __ The doves are
The doves are soar - ing, __ The doves are

sky, __ three doves __ are fly - ing, __ In the sky, _____ three doves are
sea, __ the doves __ are go - ing, __ O'er the sea, _____ the doves are
wings, __ the doves __ are soar - ing, __ On white wings, _____ the doves are

fly - ing, ___
go - ing, ___
soar - ing, ___

Ah‧___

F   C   G₇   C

fly - ing, ___   Hear their haunt - ing cry, Hear their haunt-ing cry, Hear their haunt-ing cry.
go - ing, ___   To a land they know, To a land they know, To a land they know.
soar - ing, ___   To re - turn no more, To re - turn no more, To re - turn no more.

What is in the sound
of the Hebrew words
that adds to the mood?

Be You Brave

ISRAELI ROUND

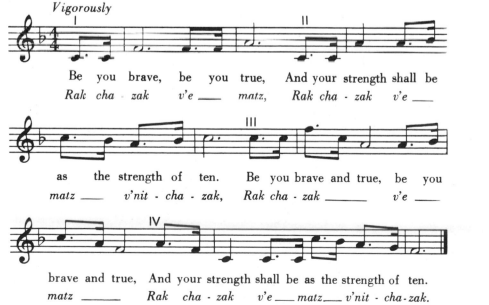

Vigorously

I

II

Be you brave, be you true, And your strength shall be
Rak cha - zak v'e ___ matz, Rak cha - zak v'e ___

III

as the strength of ten. Be you brave and true, be you
matz ___ v'nit - cha - zak, Rak cha - zak ___ v'e ___

IV

brave and true, And your strength shall be as the strength of ten.
matz ___ Rak cha - zak v'e ___ matz ___ v'nit - cha - zak.

How does
the rhythmic pattern
contribute to the mood
of this song?

In what other
kind of music
might you expect
to find this pattern?

Style in Music

The way in which we live is greatly influenced by when and where we live. The way we dress, our manner of speech, how we travel, the houses we live in—these change from time to time and place to place and determine the style of a period. Through the years, styles have changed in music as well as in other arts.

Composers reflect the style of their times. These styles are closely related to broad periods of history. About the time America was first being settled, a period of musical history known as the *Baroque* was beginning in Europe. The Baroque was characterized by vastness of proportion and splendor of detail. Here is an example of music written in the latter part of this period. How has Bach captured the spirit of the Baroque?

Now Thank We All Our God

TRANS. BY HENRY S. DRINKER
MUSIC BY JOHANN SEBASTIAN BACH

Now thank we all our God,
In all His Migh-ty Works,

With hearts and hands and voi-ces.
For-ev-er man re-joi-ces.

Who from our

mo - ther's arms,   His

boun - ty doth be - stow.

From child - hood on through life,

23

His count-less bless-ings grow.

The next musical style is called the *Classical.* One of the great composers of this period, Franz Josef Haydn, was born in 1732, the same year as George Washington. Clarity, elegance, and careful attention to form and design are characteristics of this period. Listen for these stylistic features in Haydn's "Andante Cantabile" from "String Quartet in F. Op. 3, No. 5."

Andante Cantabile

BY FRANZ JOSEF HAYDN

In the *Romantic* period that followed, the emphasis in musical style shifted to a more personal expression of emotion. Two characteristics of this period's music are rich and varied tone colors and a greatly expanded orchestra. Can you hear how Wagner's "Ride of the Valkyries" fits this romantic style?

About the turn of the twentieth century, a new style emerged, *Impressionism*. In this style, new tonal colors hint at a mood rather than stating it boldly. What impressions come to your mind as you listen to Ravel's "Enchanted Garden"?

In the music you have studied thus far, a definite style has emerged as most characteristic of each period. Today's music is developing in many directions. Composers are experimenting with diverse ideas that may eventually develop into the dominant style of our times. The new combinations of sounds and complex rhythms that you hear in Bela Bartok's "Contrasts for Violin, Clarinet, and Piano" illustrate some of the developments in contemporary music. The first performance was played by Bartok with Joseph Szigeti and Benny Goodman, to whom the work is dedicated.

Contrasts

BY BELA BARTOK

As you listen to and sing the songs on the following pages, decide which style and period each represents.

Voi Che Sapete

FROM "THE MARRIAGE OF FIGARO"
WORDS BY LORENZO DA PONTE

Voi che sa - pe - te che co - s'e a - mor,

Don - ne, ve - de - te s'io l'ho nel cor.

Don - ne, ve - de - te, ___ s'io l'ho __ nel __ cor.

In "Voi Che Sapete," a lovesick young boy sings that he is in love with all the women in the world. In opera, a mezzo-soprano voice is often used to suggest the timbre of a boy's voice.

L'Heure Exquise

WORDS BY PAUL VERLAINE

Leger et lointain

La lu - ne blan - che

Luit   dans les bois;   De cha - que bran - che Part u - ne

Below are the complete French and English texts for "L'Heure Exquise."

La lune blanche	The silver moon
Luit dans les bois;	Streams in the woods.
De chaque branche	From ev'ry branch
Part une voix	Murmurs a voice
Sous la ramée	Soft as a sigh
O bienaimée.	O, my beloved.
L'étang reflète,	The pool reflects
Profond miroir	Like a dark mirror
La silhouette	The silhouette
Du saule noir	Of the black column
Ou le vent pleure	Where the wind weeps.
Rêvons, c'est l'heure!	Dream on...It is the hour!
Un vaste et tendre	A great and tender
Apaisement,	Soulful peace
Semble descendre	Seems to come down
Du firmament	From the heavens
Que l'astre irise.	Like a starry iris.
C'est l'heure exquise.	It is the hour of ecstasy.

Resolution

WORDS BY CHARLES IVES

Walk - ing strong - er un - der dis - tant skies,

Faith e'en needs to mark the sen - ti - men - tal pla - ces; Who

can tell where Truth may ap - pear, to guide the journ - ey!

The Two Grenadiers

WORDS BY HEINE
MUSIC BY ROBERT SCHUMANN

The song begins like a sturdy march. However, by following the words, you soon learn that the two grenadiers are not going to war but returning from a prisoner-of-war camp, sad and dejected. The march music is merely a reminder of past glory, and is heard several times throughout the first part of the song. As the first soldier speaks of his desire to be buried in France, the music becomes more and more agitated. The excitement continues to mount, until, at the words, "I will quietly lie and listen," the music bursts into "La Marseillaise," the French national anthem (see page 59). Gradually the excitement dies down and a few quiet chords at the conclusion of the song seem to tell us that the soldier has only been dreaming about once more fighting for his beloved emperor, Napoleon.

(see page 59)

Nach Frankreich zogen zwei Grenadier',
Die waren in Russland gefangen.
Und als sie kamen in's deutsche Quartier,
Sie liessen die Köpfe hangen.

Towards France, wearily walked two grenadiers
Who had been imprisoned in Russia.
And as they crossed into Germany,
Their heads hung listlessly.

Da hörten sie Beide die traurige Mähr':
Dass Frankreich verloren gegangen,
Besiegt und geschlagen das tapfere Herr
Und der Kaiser, der Kaiser gefangen.

There both heard the sad news;
That France had been defeated,
Its brave men attacked and killed,
And the Emperor, the Emperor imprisoned!

Da weinten zusammen die Grenadier'
Wohl ob der kläglichen Kunde.
Der Eine sprach: "Wie weh', wird mir,
Wie brennt meine alte Wunde!"

The two Grenadiers wept together
At hearing such sorrowful news.
One said, "It's just as painful
As ever my old wounds were."

Der Andre sprach: "Das Lied ist aus,
Auch ich möcht' mit dir sterben,
Doch hab' ich Weib und Kind zu Haus,
Die ohne mich verderben."

The other spoke, "It's ended now.
Gladly would I die with you,
But I have a wife and child at home
Who cannot survive without me."

"Was schert mich Weib, was schert mich Kind,
Ich trage weit besser Verlangen;
Lass sie betteln gehn, wenn sie hungrig sind—
Mein Kaiser, Mein Kaiser gefangen!

"What matters wife, what matters child?
I bear a much greater sorrow.
Let them go begging if they're hungry...
My Emperor, my Emperor imprisoned!

Gewähr' mir, Bruder, eine Bitt':
Wenn ich jetzt sterben werde,
So nimm meine Leiche nach Frankreich mit,
Begrab' mich in Frankreichs Erde.

"Grant me, brother, one request.
If I must die now,
Take my body to France
And lay me in French soil.

Das Ehrenkreuz am rothen Band
Sollst du auf's Herz mir legen;
Die Flinte gieb mir in die Hand,
Und gürt' mir um den Degen.

"The medal of honor with its ribbon of red
Must you place across my heart.
My rifle put in my hand,
And buckle my sword around me.

So will ich liegen und horchen still,
Wie eine Schildwach', im Grabe,
Bis einst ich höre Kanonengebrüll
Und wiehernder Rosse Getrabe.

"I will quietly lie and listen
(As on sentry duty) in my grave,
Until I hear the cannons' roar
And the trotting, neighing horses.

Dann reitet mein Kaiser wohl über mein Grab,
Viel Schwerter klirren und blitzen,
Viel Schwerter klirren und blitzen;
Dann steig' ich gewaffnet hervor aus dem Grab
Den Kaiser, den Kaiser zu schützen!"

"And when my Emperor rides over my grave,
And swords clatter and flash,
And swords clatter and flash,
I shall rise from my grave with my weapons at hand
My Emperor, my Emperor to guard!"

1600 1610 1620 1630 1640 1650 1660 1670 1680 1690 1700 1710 1720 1730 1740 1750 1760 1770 1780 1790

BAROQUE PERIOD 1600-1760   *CLASSICAL PERIOD 1760-1820*

MUSIC   ## MUSIC

1567 ___ MONTEVERDI 1643
    1632 ___ LULLY 1687
      1659 ___ PURCELL 1695
      1653 ___ CORELLI 1713
        1668 ___ COUPERIN 1733
        1676 ___ VIVALDI 1741
        1685 ___ BACH 1750
        1685 ___ HANDEL 1759
        1685 ___ SCARLATTI 1757

1756 ___ MOZART 1791
1732 ___ HAYDN
1714 ___ GLUCK 1787
1770 ___

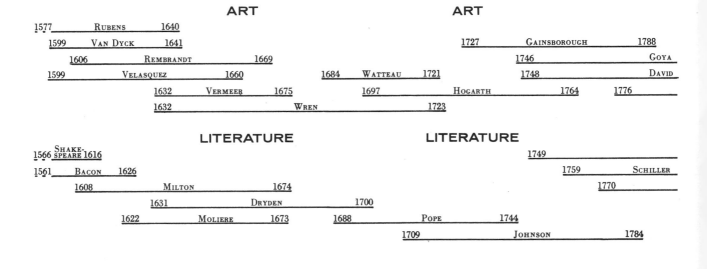

ART   ## ART

1577 ___ RUBENS 1640
1599 ___ VAN DYCK 1641
  1606 ___ REMBRANDT 1669
1599 ___ VELASQUEZ 1660
    1632 ___ VERMEER 1675
    1632 ___ WREN 1723
1684 ___ WATTEAU 1721
1697 ___ HOGARTH 1764

1727 ___ GAINSBOROUGH 1788
1746 ___ GOYA
1748 ___ DAVID
1776 ___

LITERATURE   ## LITERATURE

1566 ___ SHAKESPEARE 1616
1561 ___ BACON 1626
  1608 ___ MILTON 1674
    1631 ___ DRYDEN 1700
  1622 ___ MOLIERE 1673
1688 ___ POPE 1744
1709 ___ JOHNSON 1784

1749 ___
1759 ___ SCHILLER
1770 ___

HISTORY   ## HISTORY

Rise of European State System   *Age of Enlightenment   Revolutionary Period*

1599 ___ CROMWELL 1658
  1638 ___ LOUIS XIV 1715
  1672 ___ PETER THE GREAT 1725
    1710 ___ LOUIS XV 1774
    1712 ___ FREDERICK THE GREAT 1786
    1732 ___ WASHINGTON
    1706 ___ FRANKLIN 1790
1743 ___ JEFFERSON
1769 ___ NAPOLEON

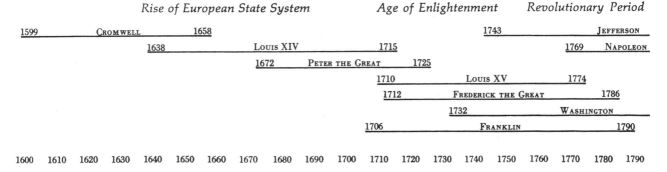

1600 1610 1620 1630 1640 1650 1660 1670 1680 1690 1700 1710 1720 1730 1740 1750 1760 1770 1780 1790

32

1790 1800 1810 1820 1830 1840 1850 1860 1870 1880 1890 1900 1910 1920 1930 1940 1950 1960 1970 1980

ROMANTIC PERIOD 1820–1900

MODERN PERIOD 1900–

MUSIC

MUSIC

1797 SCHUBERT 1828
1840 TCHAIKOVSKY 1893 1895 HINDEMITH 1964
1809 1810 CHOPIN 1849 1881 BARTOK 1945
1843 GRIEG 1907
BEETHOVEN 1827 1862 DEBUSSY 1918
1810 SCHUMANN 1856 1898 GERSHWIN 1937
1811 LISZT 1886 1900 COPLAND
1858 PUCCINI 1924
1826 FOSTER 1864 1873 RACHMANINOFF 1943
1803 BERLIOZ 1869 1874 IVES 1954
1813 WAGNER 1883 1891 PROKOFIEV 1953
1813 VERDI 1901
1833 BRAHMS 1897
1875 RAVEL 1937
1874 SCHOENBERG 1951
1882 STRAVINSKY

ART

ART

1796 COROT 1875 1881 PICASSO
1828 1853 VAN GOGH 1890 1896 WOOD 1942
1825 1834 WHISTLER 1903 1904 DALI
CONSTABLE 1837 1839 CEZANNE 1906 1917 WYETH
1798 DELACROIX 1863 1869 MATISSE 1954

LITERATURE

LITERATURE

GOETHE 1832 1875 MANN 1955
1805 1806 LONGFELLOW 1882 1888 O'NEILL 1953
WORDSWORTH 1850 1866 WELLS 1946
1792 SHELLEY 1822 1828 IBSEN 1926
1795 KEATS 1821 1875 MASEFIELD
1788 BYRON 1824 1878 SANDBURG
1812 DICKENS 1870 1874 FROST 1963
1809 TENNYSON 1892
1803 EMERSON 1882
1819 WHITMAN 1892

HISTORY

HISTORY

Industrial Revolution   *Growth of Democracy*   *Automation*   *Space Age*

1826 1882 ROOSEVELT 1945
1821 1890 EISENHOWER
1796 CZAR NICHOLAS 1855 1870 LENIN 1924
1809 LINCOLN 1865 1871 CHURCHILL 1965
1819 VICTORIA 1901 1917 KENNEDY 1963
1799 1807 GARIBALDI 1882 1889 HITLER 1945
1815 BISMARCK 1898
1803 NAPOLEON III 1873 1890 DE GAULLE

1790 1800 1810 1820 1830 1840 1850 1860 1870 1880 1890 1900 1910 1920 1930 1940 1950 1960 1970 1980

Tone and Timbre

Sound is anything we hear. What sounds do you hear right now? Some may be high, some low—some may be soft, some loud—some long, some short. Some may be noise (screeching brakes) and some may be musical tones (a church bell ringing). Distinguishing music from noise depends on many things.

1. *Pitch*

Sound is produced by setting air in motion. This is vibration. Some vibrations are faster than others. The faster the vibrations, the higher the pitch—the slower the vibrations, the lower the pitch. When the vibrations are regular or even, a musical tone results. When the vibrations are irregular or uneven, noise occurs. Strike a high key on the piano. The vibrations are fast. Strike a low key. The vibrations are slow. Below is an electronic picture of sound waves, showing low and high pitches.

Low   High

2. *Intensity*

The wider the vibration, the louder the sound. Here is an electronic picture of the same tone played loudly, then softly.

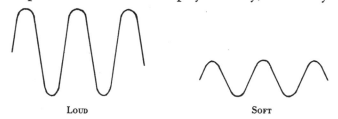

Loud   Soft

3. *Duration*

The length of a musical tone. This is a picture of the same tone with different durations.

Long   Short

4. *Timbre (tone color)*

The characteristic sound of an instrument or voice. A violin, a flute and a soprano voice can produce tones which are the same in pitch, intensity, and duration but they do not sound alike. The tone quality is determined by the size, shape, and material (metal, wood, strings, vocal chords) of the tone producing body.

VIOLIN   FLUTE   SOPRANO VOICE

Listen to the melody of Rachmaninoff's "Vocalise," as played first on the flute, then the violin, and as sung by a soprano voice. Note the different timbre of each. When you listen to music, try to understand why the composer has chosen the timbre of a particular instrument to express his musical ideas and feelings.

You have just heard a woodwind instrument, a string instrument, and a human voice; all different in timbre. The brass instruments have a still different timbre.

Before 1600, music was performed mainly by voices and instruments were used to accompany the singers. One of the first composers to write for a group of instruments playing alone was Giovanni Gabrielli (1555–1612). His "Sonata Pian' e Forte," for brass ensemble was written to be performed in the vast spaces of St. Mark's Cathedral in Venice. The strong, sustained tones of brass instruments are especially suitable for music to be heard in a large building or public square. The instruments were divided into two groups and placed on opposite sides of the church or square. As you listen, you will hear how they seem to throw the music back and forth, like a question and answer. This style is called *antiphonal*. "Sonata Pian' e Forte" means "Sounds Soft and Loud." Listen for the contrast of soft and loud passages and the distinctive timbre of the brass instruments.

While by My Sheep

TRANS. BY THEODORE BAKER
MUSIC FROM TRIER GESANGBUCH

The Christmas carol, "While by My Sheep," makes use of loud and soft (echo) effects for vocal antiphony.

Allegro Moderato

While by my sheep I watched at night, Glad ti - dings brought an an - gel bright.
Als ich bei mei - nen Scha - fen wacht, Ein En - gel mir die Bot - schaft bracht.

How great my joy, great my joy. Joy, joy, joy, Joy, joy, joy!
Des bin ich froh, bin ich froh. Froh, froh, froh, Froh, froh, froh!

Praise to the Lord in Heav'n on high. Praise to the Lord in Heav'n on high.
Be - ne - di - ca - mus Do - mi - no. Be - ne - di - ca - mus Do - mi - no.

Andante

BY LUDWIG VAN BEETHOVEN

Beethoven's "Octet for Winds, Op. 103" shows the tone color of the woodwind instruments; oboe, clarinet, bassoon, and French horn — a brass instrument often used with woodwinds because its tone color blends so well with theirs.

Andante

Hn. in B♭

Ob.

Cl. in B♭

Bsn.

In Beethoven's "Octet for Winds," you have heard the character-istic timbre of various wind instruments playing together in a small group. In the song on the next page, you will hear the timbre of solo woodwind instruments in combination with voices and piano. As you listen to the contrasting timbres, remember that although the vibrating bodies of voices and winds are different, all are dependent on breath to produce and sustain a pitch. What other group of instruments also depends on breathing to produce and sustain tone?   How does a piano produce tone?

Desert Flower

WORDS BY RENE MARTIN
NORTH AFRICAN MELODY

In the North African song, "Desert Flower," two solo woodwind instruments play an obbligato as the voice sings the melody. As you listen to the recording, try to recognize and identify the instruments by their timbre.

Warm   winds of my des - ert __ land, Send words of   love _ be - yond the drift-ing sand;

Warm winds of   my   des - ert __ land, Send words of   love be - yond the   sand;

Hear my cry, As - mar El __ Loun, Oh, __ love - ly flow - er of my lone - ly des - ert land.

Hear my cry, As - mar El __ Loun, Oh, __ flow - er of my des - ert land. *Fine*

1. Be not still as stars in Heav - en, Be not slow as the wea - ry cam-el's pace;
2. Here, be - side the Nile's dark wa - ters, I a - wait the ris - ing moon;

Bring her fra - grance, sweet as jas - mine, Let my eyes be - hold __ her face.
Fair - est one of Is - lam's daugh-ters, Come to me, As - mar __ El __ Loun.

Prelude to Act III

BY GIUSEPPE VERDI

In the "Prelude" to the last act of "La Traviata," Verdi wanted to create a mood of loneliness and sadness before the curtain went up. Here are the opening measures arranged for piano.

What instruments does Verdi use to play these measures? Does he use a high or low range? How would you describe the tone color of these instruments?

One Tone

WORDS AND MUSIC
BY PETER CORNELIUS
TRANS. BY C. HUGO LAUBACH

The meaning of the word, "monotone" is "one tone." Notice that the melody of "One Tone" is made up of the repeated tone, G. The mood is set by the harmonies in the piano part.

I hear a tone so won-drous rare; It fills my
Mir klingt ein Ton so wun-der-bar in Herz und

heart, it's ev - er there. _____ Ah, can it
Sin-nen im-mer-dar. _____ Ist es der

40

be the last faint breath That stirred your pal-lid lips in death?＿＿＿＿

Hauch, der dir ent-schwebt, als ein-mal noch dein Mund ge-bebt?＿＿＿＿

Is it the ten-der mon-o-tone Of church-bells

Ist es des Glöck-leins trü-ber Klang, der dir ge-

which for you did moan?   Lo, still it comes, so full, so

folgt den Weg ent-lang? Mir klingt der Ton so voll und

clear, As though your soul were float - ing near,＿＿＿＿

rein, als schlöss er dei-ne See - le ein,＿＿＿＿

As though with love and yearn-ing deep You sang my bit-ter pain to
als stie - gest lie - bend nie - der Du und säng-est mei - nen Schmerz in

sleep! _____
Ruh! _____

Awake!

WORDS BY CLAUDIA REGEN
MUSIC BY RICHARD WAGNER

In contrast to the repeated-note melody of "One Tone," the chorale, "Awake," from Wagner's "Die Meistersinger," uses four independent vocal lines of great complexity and extremely wide range. Many voices blending together in a large chorus have a very different tone color from a solo voice.

A - wake! The_ gold - en day_ draws near; From slow - ly bright - 'ning

woods — I hear the song ____ of a night-in-gale; Her
voice — is heard — o'er hill and — dale; The moon now fades in — west-ern skies, the
sun a-bove — the — clouds — will — rise, And dawn, glow-ing in the
mist-y air Will — greet the day — so won-drous fair.

What words would you use to describe
the mood and tone color of "Awake"?

O Vos Omnes

TEXT FROM "LAMENTATIONS"
MUSIC BY TOMAS LUIS DE VITTORIA

Much vocal music is *polyphonic* (many voices moving independently at the same time). Vittoria's "O Vos Ommes" is written for four solo voices. The difference in vocal tone colors will help you recognize each melody as it is sung.

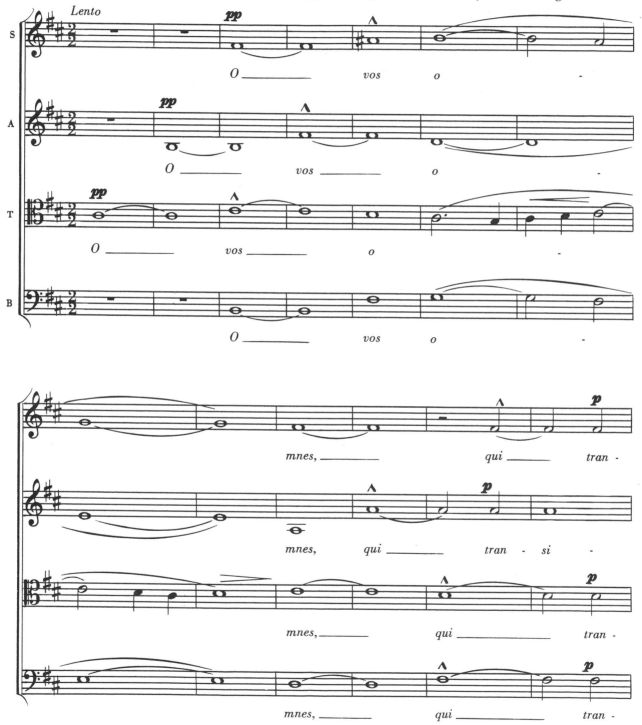

44

The text of "O Vos Omnes" is taken from the Lamentations of Jeremiah. It may be translated "Is it nothing to you, all ye that pass by." The text and music are used in church services to express the sufferings of Christ on the cross.

Oh, No, John

ENGLISH FOLK SONG

Listen to the contrasting timbre of voices singing in unison and then in three parts.

Tree by the Sea

WORDS BY MARCELLA BANNON
FRENCH FOLK TUNE

Gaily

SOLO VOICE (OR SMALL GROUP)

mp You were so fan-cy-free,

mf As I walked by the sea,

A love-ly sight to see,

I came up-on a tree,

A ver-y pret-ty tree. So high and near the sky,

A ver-y pret-ty tree. In-to its branch-es high,

Clouds were pass-ing by, It was so ex - qui - site Near the sky to sit and sigh,

Went I to sit and sigh, O my!

A love - ly sight to see, The tree by the bright blue sea.

I sat in the pret - ty tree, The tree by the bright blue sea.

For variety of timbre, this song has been arranged with baritones singing melody and a special upper part for changing voices.

Big Corral

TRADITIONAL COWBOY SONG

Cheerfully

Ti yip- pee yay,____ Ti yip- pee yay,____

Press a - long,

MELODY

1. That big hus - ky brute from the cat - tle chute, } Press a - long, to the Big Cor -
2. The food we got is - n't fit to eat,

Press a - long cow - boy,

ral,

He should be brand - ed on the snoot, } Press a -
There's rocks in the beans and sand in the meat,

To the Big Cor - ral, yip - pee yay! Press a - long,

long, to the Big Cor - ral, yip - pee yay! Press a long,

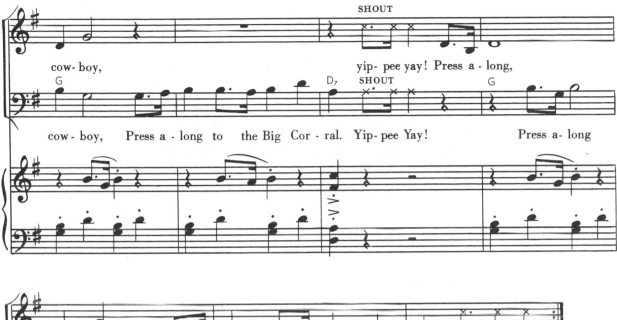

SHOUT

cow- boy, yip- pee yay! Press a - long,

G D₇ SHOUT G

cow- boy, Press a - long to the Big Cor - ral. Yip- pee Yay! Press a- long

cow- boy, Press a - long to the Big Cor - ral. Yip- pee Yay!

G A₇ D₇ G

cow- boy, Press a - long, to the Big Cor - ral Yip- pee Yay!

THE DROVER

Move 'em out! goes the cry,
And the herd's on the run,
The cowboys are punchin'—
The long ride's begun.

Hit 'em up! It's a shout,
Or a song, or a word,
When the dust settles down,
Then we quiet the herd.

Bring 'em in! calls the drover,
It's time for a rest;
And another trek's over
Out here in the west.
—MARC RICHARDS

La Soirée dans Grenade

FROM "ESTAMPES"
BY CLAUDE DEBUSSY

"La Soiree dans Grenade" is a tonal picture of an evening in Granada, a city in southern Spain. Granada was the center of the Moorish culture in Spain, and it is amazing how Debussy, who never really visited Spain, captures and combines the Spanish and Moorish character.

The tempo indication is "rhythm of a habanera" and this rhythm runs through the entire piece as a unifying idea. Listen to the opening measures where the habanera rhythm is played high on the piano (sounding like the tiny, silver bells worn by donkeys in Spain) and combined with an exotic, Moorish-style melody. The music below (from the conclusion of the piece) combines these musical ideas but adds rich chords for a feeling of completion.

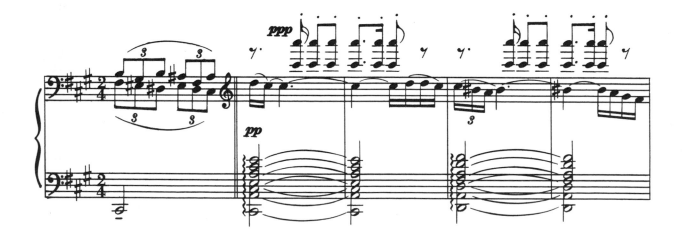

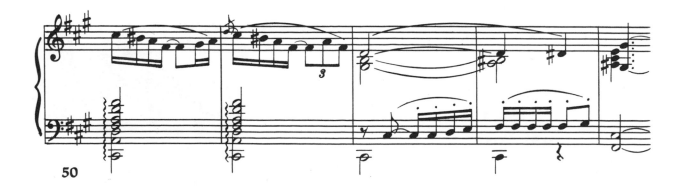

50

Item for Percussion

BY SAUL FELDSTEIN

As you listen to the recording, you will hear a B section. How would you describe the contrasting timbre of the two sections?

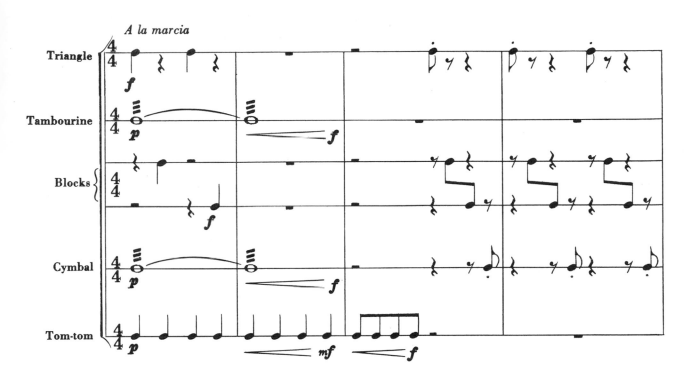

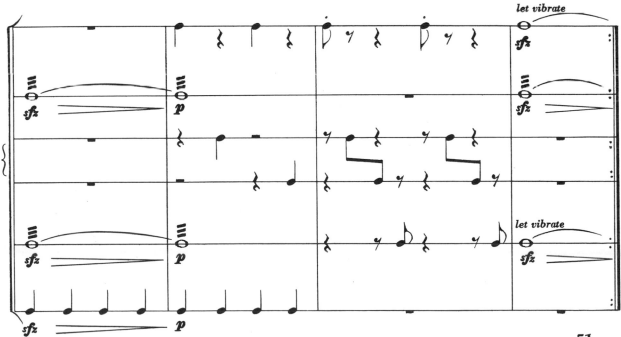

Form in Music

Everything has form. There is form in nature—the shape of a tree, the arc of a rainbow, the pattern of a butterfly's wing. Other forms are man made—the structure of a building, the span of a bridge, the design of a painting. When we sing, play, or listen to music, we discover that music also has various forms. In this chapter, we shall explore some of these forms as they are used in music.

One of the simpler forms of music is the *leader-response* or *question-answer*. The folk song, "Whistle, Mary, Whistle" is one example of this form.

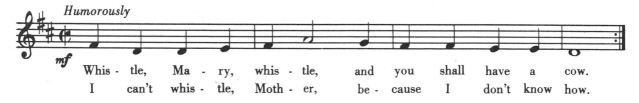

Humorously

Whis - tle, Ma - ry, whis - tle, and you shall have a cow.
I can't whis - tle, Moth - er, be - cause I don't know how.

Like most folk songs, "Whistle, Mary, Whistle," has many verses and could easily become monotonous when repeated over and over. What has the arranger done to make the song more interesting and to highlight the form?

Whistle, Mary, Whistle

AMERICAN FOLK SONG

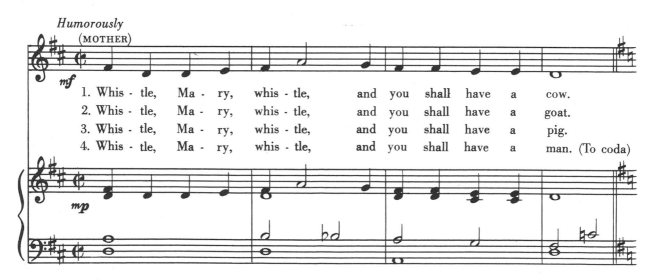

Humorously
(MOTHER)

1. Whis - tle, Ma - ry, whis - tle, and you shall have a cow.
2. Whis - tle, Ma - ry, whis - tle, and you shall have a goat.
3. Whis - tle, Ma - ry, whis - tle, and you shall have a pig.
4. Whis - tle, Ma - ry, whis - tle, and you shall have a man. (To coda)

52

1. I can't whis-tle, moth-er, be-cause I don't know how.
2. I can't whis-tle, moth-er, be-cause it hurts my throat.
3. I can't whis-tle, moth-er, be-cause I am too big.

Coda

(DAUGHTER)

I've just found out I can.

4. *(Whistle)* _____

(MOTHER)

-She's just found out she can.

The next song, "Old Man Noah," includes the *leader-response* idea. Where do you find it? The first part of the song is the verse, which we call section A. The refrain, or contrasting section, is called B. The design is called A-B or *two-part form*.

Old Man Noah

SEA CHANTEY

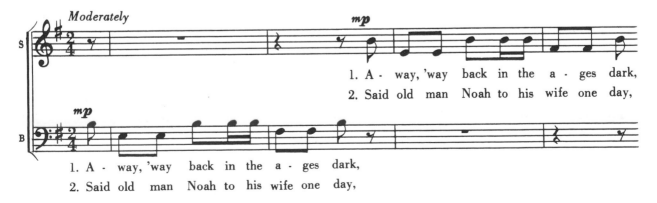

1. A - way, 'way back in the a - ges dark,
2. Said old man Noah to his wife one day,

1. A - way, 'way back in the a - ges dark,
2. Said old man Noah to his wife one day,

Old man No-ah knew a thing or two, Be-cause he knew a thing or two, he

thought he knew it all. Some say he was an "al-so ran." He was th'o-rig-i-nal

cir-cus man. Old man No-ah knew a thing or two; He was a grand old man.

What is the form of the next song?

Still, Still, Still

TRANS. BY MARY DUTRE
GERMAN CAROL

Moderato

mp Still, ___ still, ___ still, The ___ In-fant ___ Je-sus ___ sleeps;
Still, ___ still, ___ still, Weil's ___ Kind-lein ___ schlaf-en ___ will.

How ten-der-ly His Moth-er ___ holds Him, Near to her heart how gent-ly she folds Him
Ma-ri-a ___ tut es nie-der ___ sing-en, Ih-re ___ keu-sche Brust dar-bring-en,

Still, ___ still, ___ still, The ___ In-fant ___ Je-sus ___ sleeps.
Still, ___ still, ___ still, Weil's ___ Kind-lein ___ schlaf-en ___ will.

55

Autumn Voices

WORDS BY M. A. DUFAY
FINNISH FOLK MELODY

You have discovered that the phrases of "Still, Still, Still" are in A-B-A form. In "Autumn Voices," each section of the A-B-A is lengthened. How has this been done?

S Voi - ces of the au - tumn winds, Through the mists are call - ing,

A Voi - ces of the au - tumn winds, Through the

Sing fare - well to a sum - mer's go - ing When the leaves are fall - ing.

mists are call - ing, Sing fare - well to a sum - mer's go - ing When the

Mur - mur of the crick - ets' wings, In the mea - dow grass - es,

leaves are fall - ing. Mur - mur of the crick - ets' wings, In the

Hum fare - well to a fad - ing flow - er As the sum - mer pass - es.

mea - dow grass - es, Hum fare - well to a fad - ing flow - er As the sum - mer pass - es.

Rest, un - til the dark clouds light - en. Rest, un - til the dawn - ing.

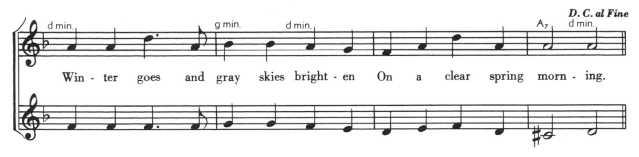

Win - ter goes and gray skies bright - en On a clear spring morn - ing.

What are some of the differences between the A and B sections?

A-B-A is one of the most frequently used song forms, especially with the first section repeated—A-A-B-A. Does "Let A Smile Be Your Umbrella" follow this form? Is it A-B-A or A-A-B-A?

Let a Smile be Your Umbrella

WORDS BY IRVING KAHAL AND FRANCIS WHEELER
MUSIC BY SAMMY FAIN

Just let a smile be your um-brel-la on a rain-y, rain-y day,___

And if your sweet-ie cries just tell her that a smile will al-ways pay.___

When-ev-er skies are gray don't wor-ry or fret,___

A smile will bring the sun-shine and you'll nev-er get wet,___

So let a smile be your um-brel-la on a rain-y, rain-y day!___

Some songs achieve balance without having any repeated phrases or sections. This form may be called *chain-of-phrases*. A familiar example is "America." Another song in this form is "La Marseillaise."

La Marseillaise

WORDS AND MUSIC
BY ROUGET DE LISLE
TRANS. BY ALAN WILLS

Vigorously

Ye sons of France, a - wake to glo - ry, The peo - ple bid you to a - rise!
Al - lons, en - fants de la pa - tri - e, Le jour de gloire est ar - ri - vé

With sword un - sheathed go for - ward to bat - tle, Soon the ty - rant shall be de - stroyed,
Con - tre nous de la ty - ran - ni - e L'é - ten - dard san - glant est le - vé!

And the ty - rant shall soon be de - stroyed. Go for - ward with your friends and com - pan - ions
L'é - ten - dard __ san - glant est le - vé! En - ten - dez vous __ dans les cam - pa - gnes

To a - venge your dear na - tive land. The time for bat - tle is at hand;
Mu - gir ces fé - ro - ces sol - dats? Ils vien - nent jus - que dans nos bras

Hear the cries of your wives and of your chil - dren. To arms __ ye sons of France!
E - gor - ger __ nos fils, __ nos com - pa - gnes! Aux ar - mes, ci - toy - ens!

Fight on __ to vic - to - ry! __ March on, march on!
For - mez __ vos ba - tail - lons! __ Mar - chons, mar - chons!

All hearts re - solved on vic - to - ry or death! __
Qu'un sang im - pur a - breu - ve nos sil - lons! __

In music, well-balanced forms are achieved through
repetition, variation, and contrast.

Lament

FROM "CAPRICCIO ON THE DEPARTURE OF A BELOVED BROTHER"
BY JOHANN SEBASTIAN BACH

This is an unusual work for Bach because it is an example of *program music*—music that has a descriptive title and is often inspired by a story, poem, or historical event. In this case, the "program" is based on an actual event in Bach's life; the departure of his older brother, Johann Jacob, to serve as an oboist with the Swedish Guard. The titles of the movements are listed below.

1. His friends coax him to give up his journey.

2. They describe the dangers of the trip.

3. General lament of his friends.

4. Seeing it cannot be otherwise, the friends say goodby.

5. Aria of the postilion.

6. Fugue in imitation of the postilion's horn.

It is the third movement, marked *Adagissimo* (very slow), that we will hear. Like the "Passacaglia in C minor," it is made up of variations written above a descending bass line. Here are the first four measures. What mood do they create?

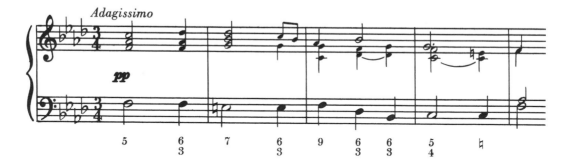

You will notice in the first musical example that there are numbers under the bass notes. This notation is called *figured bass*, and indicates the notes to be played above the bass. For example, the 5 under the first note tells us to play the note a *fifth* above the bass. This note (C) appears in the top part, and, with the bass part outlines a I chord (F-Ab-C) in the key of f minor. (The Ab will be found in the alto part and the bass F is doubled in the tenor part.) Playing from figured bass was expected of all musicians in Bach's time. However, the figures indicated only the general chords to be used. How the notes were arranged was left to the taste and imagination of the performer. The example at the top of the next page is taken from the middle of the "Lament." Note the use of chromaticism to show sorrow.

Passacaglia in C minor

BY JOHANN SEBASTIAN BACH

The word, passacaglia, originally meant a street dance. It is derived from two Spanish words: *passar* (to walk) and *calle* (street). As used in music, passacaglia means a composition in *theme and variation form*. The passacaglia theme or melody appears in the bass and is repeated over and over (as an *ostinato*) while a series of variations is played above it. The theme for Bach's famous "Passacaglia in C minor" is eight measures long, and extends over an octave and a sixth.

Adagio

To establish the melody clearly in your mind, sing it on "loo." Girls and boys with unchanged voices will sing an octave higher. You will not be able to sing the last three low tones, but your teacher will help you sing them an octave higher. It will also help if you listen carefully to the theme as it is played several times on the piano. You will have no problem hearing the theme on the recording since it is first heard by itself without any variations above. After the theme is played, we hear a series of twenty variations of great variety and beauty. Some are light and delicate. Some are strong and overwhelmingly powerful. Although a true passacaglia always has the melody in the bass part, you will notice that Bach uses it in the middle and upper registers of the organ. Sometimes it is subdued, but it is always heard throughout the composition.

Bach wrote the "Passacaglia in C minor" around 1715. As was often the custom of the period, Bach "borrowed" the first four measures of this bass theme from a *Trio en passacaille* by Andre Raison, a French organist of the 17th century.

61

Variations on "Ah, Vous dirais-je, Maman"

BY WOLFGANG AMADEUS MOZART

The melody Mozart used for these twelve variations for piano is familiar to all of you. See if you can identify the melody of the theme from the notation.

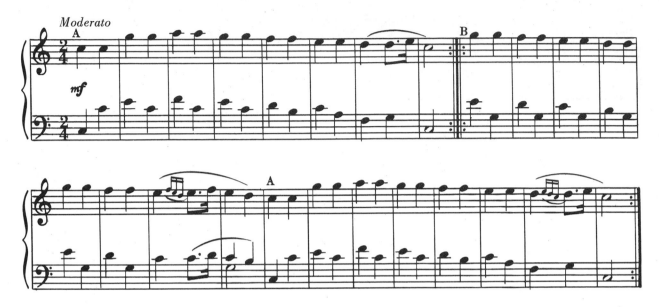

If you are unable to do so, you will certainly recognize the melody as your teacher plays it on the piano.

You will observe that in the theme the musical design is: A (8 measures), A (repeated); B (8 measures), followed by A (8 measures) with both B and A repeated. The form, then, is A A B A B A. Notice how this pattern is followed in each of the variations.

Since the basic idea for each variation, once it is established by Mozart, is carried on throughout the variation, we are quoting only the first four measures of the variations appearing in your book. In the first variation, notice how the first two melody notes (C C) are embellished with *upper and lower neighboring* tones (*D C B C B C B* C) in the sixteenth note figuration in the upper part.

In variation 2, Mozart elaborates the bass line with upper and lower neighboring tones, much as he embellished the melody tones in the first variation. In the third variation, a triplet figure is used for still another way to change the melody in the right hand. (You will recall that a triplet is a three-note pattern played in the time usually occupied by only two notes having the same value.)

In variation 4, Mozart uses the triplet pattern in the left hand or bass part. Variation 5 is an antiphonal echoing of the melody between the two hands.

The sixth variation has the melody in the top note of the detached chords in the treble staff. The seventh variation begins with an extended scale pattern—two octaves of the C major scale followed by left hand octaves and "broken" note patterns in the right hand.

In variation 8, we have our first change of key; from C major to c minor. Notice the contrapuntal effect achieved by the left hand answering in measure 3 what the right hand began in measure 1.

The ninth variation also uses this contrapuntal idea but has a completely different character. Notice that the music has returned to the key of C major.

In variation 10, the melody, high in the treble, is played by crossing the left hand over the right. What are some of the musical means Mozart uses for variety in variation 11?

Variation 12 serves as a finale. What do you hear and see in the music that gives a feeling of finality?

Minuet and Trio

FROM "SYMPHONY NO. 39, IN E♭"
BY WOLFGANG AMADEUS MOZART

The *minuet and trio* is often found as the third movement of the classical symphony, particularly those of Haydn and Mozart. The minuet is a stately court dance in triple meter. The trio is so-called because it was the practice in the 17th century to write minuets and other dances for three different instruments. In symphonic writing, it usually means a smaller ensemble of instruments.

Mozart's "Minuet and Trio" may be outlined as follows:

MINUET
    Theme A, *(repeated)*
    Theme B, Theme A, *(both repeated)*

TRIO
    Theme C, *(repeated)*
    Theme D, Theme C, *(both repeated)*

MINUET
    Theme A,
    Theme B, Theme A.

Colonel Bogey March

BY KENNETH J. ALFORD

Kenneth J. Alford is often referred to as the "English Sousa." His marches have much the same stirring, rhythmic flavor associated with the marches of John Philip Sousa (see pages 138-139 and 171).

The first melody (or first "strain") is very brisk; made up of short, detached motives. It is immediately repeated in its entirety. As you listen, try to identify the instruments you hear.

The second melody (or "strain") contrasts greatly with the first melody. What instruments play the second melody?

What gives it a feeling of strength and driving movement? Notice that it, like the first melody, is repeated.

At this point, the first theme is heard again. It is played through once and not repeated. Following the return of the first theme, we hear the *trio*. Does it seem closer in mood to the first theme of the the second theme? It begins *piano* and builds to a *forte* climax. After the trio, there is a final return to the first theme and the march ends vigorously.

If we think of the first theme as section A, the second theme as section B, and the trio as section C, the form is a very clear A-B-A-C-A, or *second rondo form*. You will often hear performances of "Colonel Bogey March" in which the first melody is whistled instead of played by the band. To highlight the rondo form, whistle the melody of A each time it returns.

Rhythm in Music

Rhythm is all around us: in the ebb and flow of the tides, the rising and setting of the sun, the inhaling and exhaling of air as we breathe. The steady beating of your heart is a regular rhythm. Some rhythm is free; like the bending and swaying of trees in the wind. Can you think of other examples of regular and irregular rhythms?

Rhythm is found in all types of music. Rhythm in music is the flow of tones: their duration, their emphasis, and their grouping into recognizable patterns. In the following songs, we will explore many ways rhythm is used in music.

What rhythm pattern forms the basis for "School Song"? Compare this pattern with those found in other strongly rhythmic songs, such as "La Marseillaise" (page 59), "Heav'n," (page 120), and "Seventy-six Trombones" (page 154).

School Song

WORDS BY FRANCIS ANDERSON
GERMAN FOLK MELODY

Ev- 'ry school has a song That it sings loud and strong,
Once a-gain, loud and clear, Let the world lend an ear,

You will hear it at games When we're march-ing a-long.
When we fin-ish our song We will all give a cheer.

It's a song with a beat, Noth-ing trick-y, but it's neat,

It will lift spir - its high, It will guard a - gainst de - feat.

Which of the three meter signatures in this song is most typical of the waltz? You might make up a spoken chant in each meter for part of the class to speak as a rhythm accompaniment while the rest sing.

Start Singing

WORDS BY GILBERT COOK
GERMAN FOLK MELODY

Start sing - ing, start sing - ing, but lis - ten for one thing!
Guten A - bend, guten A - bend euch al - len hier bei - samm!

This tune looks quite eas - y but it may prove trick - y, It
Ihr Män - ner und Frau - en und Bur - schen und Mä - del, bei,

moves like a waltz now, just count up to three.
lu - stig soll's wer - den, ich spiel' euch eins auf!

A waltz moves in three - four, Now lis - ten just once more!
Streich zu auf der Fie - del, den Wal - zer spiel uns auf!

Tra la la la la la la la la, tra la la la la la la la la, tra la la la.

Me Yearee Say

WORDS ADAPTED BY JOSEPH RESOL
CARIBBEAN FOLK MELODY

CLAVES

BONGOS

SOLO

mf You year - ee wah me year - ee? ___

Calypso Tempo

mf

3. Ol' Saint Peter said, "What's doin' here?
   We've got no room this year."

4. All the men still up there flyin' round,
   Don't know when they be found.

The Rose Complaining

TRANS. BY H. G. TREBILCOX
MUSIC BY ROBERT FRANZ

What rhythmic devices help to convey
the mood of this lovely art song?

1. A love-ly rose did once com-plain,—
1. *Es hat die Ro-se sich be-klagt,—*

"I've lost my frag-rance so in-vit-ing, And Spring-time told me it would lin-ger."
dass gar zu schnell der Duft ver-ge-he, den ihr der Lenz ge-ge-ben ha-be.

POSTLUDE

2. And so I hastened to explain,
   "Your fragrance joined the song I'm writing,
   To be reborn by ev'ry singer."

2. *Da hab' ich ihr zum Trost gesagt,*
   Dass er durch meine Lieder wehe,
   Und dort ein ew'ges Leben habe.

You Can Dig My Grave

SPIRITUAL

Most spirituals are strongly rhythmic and use syncopation. Where does syncopation occur in "You Can Dig My Grave"?

MELODY

1. You can dig my grave with a sil - ver spade, You can dig my grave with a
2. There's a gold - en harp in the heav'n for me, There's a gold - en harp in the

sil - ver spade, You can dig my grave with a sil - ver spade, } 'Cause I
heav'n for me, There's a gold - en harp in the heav'n for me,

1. ain't gon - na stay here an - y long - er.   2. ain't gon - na stay here an - y long - er.

71

Three Suitors

WORDS BY CLAUDIA REGEN
LATVIAN FOLK MELODY

Why is 5/4 called an "irregular" meter? How does it differ from "regular" meters? If you listen to the second movement of Tchaikovsky's "Pathetique Symphony," you will hear an example of symphonic music written in 5/4 meter.

With motion

1. Three young broth-ers met a maid one day, And each vowed that she must go his way.
2. Said the first one, You would go through life, gai - ly sing - ing, danc - ing as my wife."

Each one told of treas - ures he'd be - stow, Each one spoke of pleas - ures she would know.
"No, no, dance and song would wea - ry me, No, no, not such end - less gai - e - ty."

3. Said the second, "Build a house I will,
   Strong and solid, high upon a hill."
   "No, no, for a prison it would be,
   No, no, keeping house is not for me."

4. Said the third one, "Sweet maid, would you care?
   I have nothing but my love to share."
   "Yes, yes, I will take the love you give,
   Yes, yes, for as long as we shall live."

Cicerenella

WORDS BY M. A. DUFAY
ITALIAN FOLK MELODY

This song is written in the rhythm of a **tarantella**, a lively dance from Italy in 3/8 or 6/8 meter.

Allegretto

CASTANETS

TAMBOURINE

DESCANT

Ah

MELODY

1. Ci - ce - re - nel - la, the gar - den - er's daugh - ter, Sprayed her gar - den with so - da and
2. Ci - ce - re - nel - la, once owned a queer don - key, Made him hats but he looked like a

Ah

wa - ter. Ci - ce - re - nel - la, the gar - den - er's daugh - ter, Sprayed her
mon - key. Ci - ce - re - nel - la once owned a queer don - key, Made him

Ah

gar - den with so - da and wa - ter. Shad - ed it all with a ti - ny um -
hats but he looked like a mon - key. She was con - vinced that he was *mol - ta*

Ah

brel - la, That was the gar - den of Ci - ce - re - nel - la. Shad - ed it
bel - la, That was the don - key of Ci - ce - re - nel - la. She was con -

Ah

all with a ti - ny um - brel - la, That was the gar - den of Ci - ce - re -
vinced that he was *mol - ta bel - la,* That was the don - key of Ci - ce - re -

Ah

nel - la.
nel - la. } Ci - ce - re - nel - la mi - a, Si bo - na e bel - la.

Give My Regards to Broadway

WORDS AND MUSIC
BY GEORGE M. COHAN

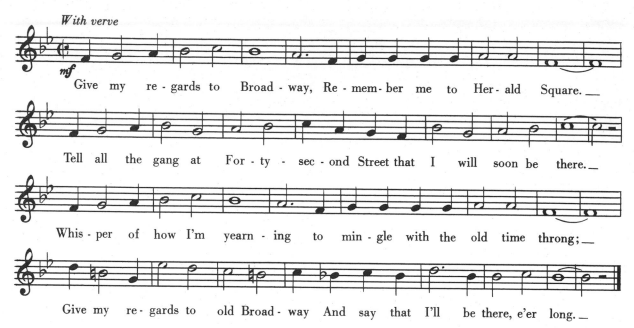

With verve

mf Give my re-gards to Broad-way, Re-mem-ber me to Her-ald Square. ___

Tell all the gang at For-ty - sec-ond Street that I will soon be there. ___

Whis - per of how I'm yearn - ing to min - gle with the old time throng; ___

Give my re-gards to old Broad-way And say that I'll be there, e'er long. ___

Sometimes I Feel Like a Motherless Child

SPIRITUAL

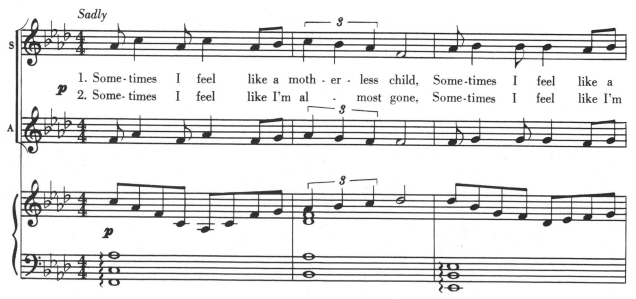

Sadly

p 1. Some-times I feel like a moth-er-less child, Some-times I feel like a
2. Some-times I feel like I'm al - most gone, Some-times I feel like I'm

74

moth - er - less child, Some-times I feel like a moth-er-less child,
al - most gone, Some-times I feel like I'm al - most gone,
A
'Way

A long ways from home.

long ways_ from home,_____ A long ways_ from home.
up in _ that heav'n-ly land, 'Way up in _ that land.

True be-liev-er, A long ways from home.
True be-liev-er, 'Way up in that land.

True be-liev-er, A long ways_ from home,_____ A long ways_ from home.
True be-liev-er,'Way up in_ that heav'n-ly land, 'Way up in _ that land.

Chickery Chick

WORDS BY SYLVIA DEE
MUSIC BY SIDNEY LIPPMAN

Are the rhythm patterns in this song similar or widely varied? Practice saying the nonsense words in rhythm until you can perform them easily.

Cheerfully

Once there lived a chick-en who would say, "Chick-chick"— "Chick-chick"— all day.

Soon that chick got sick and tired of just "Chick-chick," so one morn-ing she start-ed to say:

"Chick-er-y chick cha-la cha-la, check-a-la rome-y in a ba-nan-i-ka,

bol-li-ka wol-li-ka can't you see, Chick-er-y Chick is me.

Chick-er-y chick cha-la cha-la, check-a-la rome-y in a ba-nan-i-ka,

bol-li-ka wol-li-ka can't you see, Chick-er-y Chick is me."

Ev-'ry time you're sick and tired of just the same old thing,

Say-in' just the same old words all day, Be just like the chick-en who found

some-thing new to sing. O-pen up your mouth and start to say, Oh!

Chick-er-y chick cha-la cha-la, check-a-la rome-y in a ba-nan-i-ka,

bol-li-ka wol-li-ka can't you see, Chick-er-y Chick is me.

The traditional polka rhythm is $\frac{2}{4}$

Compare it with the rhythm patterns found in this contemporary polka. What similarities do you see?

Jumping Polka

WORDS BY HILDA HEIFETZ
MUSIC BY EMANUEL R. HEIFETZ

Briskly

(SPOKEN) 1, 2, 3, Jump!
1. Pol-kas come and pol-kas go, But there's one you won't for-get,
2. First you learn a sim-ple step, Then you take your part-ner's hand,

Once you sing it you will know It's the best one you've heard yet.
Skip a-round with lots of pep To the mu-sic of the land. 1, 2, 3, Jump!

Jump-ing Pol-ka is the name, There's nev-er been an-oth-er quite the same.

Jump-ing Pol-ka has a beat that's guar-an-teed to get you on your feet.

What do you see and hear in this melody
that gives the song
a lilting quality we associate
with a Viennese waltz?

Only You

WORDS BY H. G. TREBILCOX
MUSIC BY JOHANN STRAUSS
FROM "DIE FLEDERMAUS"

Waltz tempo

mp On - ly you, on - ly you, I've known it from the start,

On - ly you, on - ly you, Know what is in my heart;

On - ly you, on - ly you, Can be the one for me,

You are mine, on - ly you, You and I, just we two;

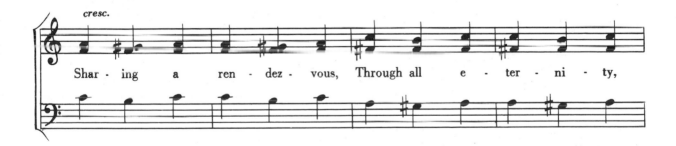

Shar - ing a ren - dez - vous, Through all e - ter - ni - ty,

You _____ are the one, on - - - ly you.

Una Valencianita

WORDS BY MARCELLA BANNON
SPANISH FOLK MELODY

The alternation of bars in 3/4 and 6/8 meter creates a very vigorous rhythmic movement. Compare "Una Valencianita" with "America," from Leonard Bernstein's "West Side Story."

Rhythmically

REFRAIN

Is - a - be -li - ta, they call me, Is - a - be - li - ta, so gay.
Is - a - be -li - ta, me lla - mo, Is - a - be - li - ta, fe - liz,

Play for me, sing to me al - ways, I will not send you a - way.
Tó - ca - me, cán - ta - me siem - pre, Y no te des - pa - char - é.

Fine

Clap
Tap

VERSE

1. *U - na - Va - len - cia - ni - ta,* Like the ro - ses of Spain,
2. For you, Va - len - cia - ni - ta, For your beau - ti - ful smile,

Love - li - est of the gar - den,   With you   I would re - main.
For your cheeks like the ro - ses,   I   will stay for a - while.

Since the first day I   saw you,   My life can't be the same,
Neath your win - dow I'm play - ing, Se - re - nad - ing my love,

Ah! sweet Va - len - cia - ni - ta,   Could I   but know your name.
I   will be as you want me,   True as   the stars a - bove.

D. C. al Fine

Making Up Rhythms

As your teacher claps the following rhythmic "question," respond by clapping an "echo answer."

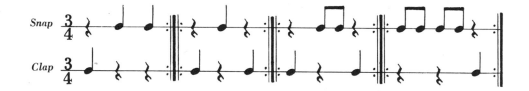

An echo answer, of course, is an exact repetition. Now make up a *different* rhythmic pattern that also answers or balances the pattern given above.

Make up your own "question" in 2/4, 3/4, or 4/4 meter. Your classmates will answer with either an exact repetition (echo) or with an original pattern. Try playing some of these question and answer patterns on rhythm instruments.

To add variety in performing rhythmic patterns, we might add stamping our feet, patting our thighs, and snapping our fingers in addition to clapping. Using a moderate tempo, try the *finger snapping-clapping* patterns you see below.

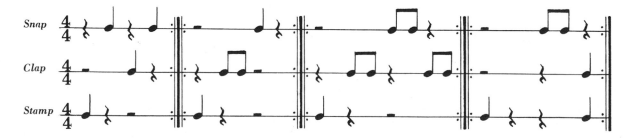

Work on each repeated measure pattern until you are able to do it well. Then read the entire four measures without repeat signs. You may wish to use claves to play the "clap" part and triangle to play the "snap" part. In the same way, work out the following *snapping-clapping-stamping* patterns.

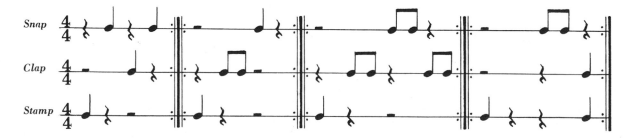

You may wish to add a drum, gong, or woodblocks on the "stamp" line. Use the claves and triangle as before.

Here is a *snapping-clapping-thigh patting-stamping* pattern.
Work it out as you did the preceding pattern.

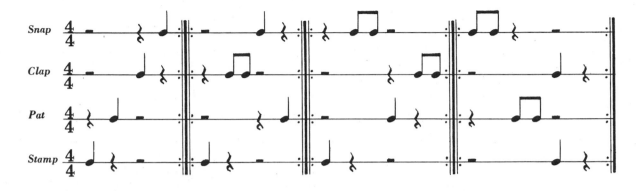

When you add instruments, use a tambourine for the "patting"
part. Use the drums, claves, and triangle as you did before.
You will, of course, get an entirely different effect if you experiment with other combinations of instruments.

Now work out some original patterns. Try
first clapping alone, then the clap-snap
effect, followed by the snap-clap-stamp.
Finally, try a snap-clap-pat-stamp pattern.
You will find that it is fun to make up patterns like these to accompany such rhythmic songs as "Water Come a' Me Eye" p.11,
"Tree By the Sea," p. 46, "In This Land,"
p. 86, "Shoo Fly," p. 116, "Tzena, Tzena,"
p. 130, and many others.

Here is a rhythm round for spoken voices. After you have
become familiar with "War Dance," you may wish to score it
for percussion instruments or for some of the body movements
we have used in the earlier patterns.

War Dance

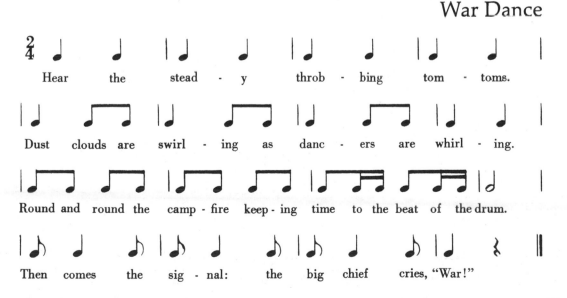

A *rhythm rondo* is an extension of the question and answer idea. You will remember that the simplest form of a rondo is A-B-A-C-A. If we regard A as our question, we have two different answers, B and C. Below is the A section for a rhythm rondo. Make up first a B answer and then a C answer. Finally, play the entire rhythm rondo in A-B-A-C-A form.

The A section above is performed by the entire class. For variety, the B and C sections should be performed by a soloist or a small group of players. Can you think of other ways that you might add contrast between the A section and the B and C sections? Try making up your own A section in a different meter and develop an entirely new rhythm rondo. Play it on percussion instruments.

Bolero

BY MAURICE RAVEL

A *bolero* (from the Spanish *volar*, "to fly") is a very dramatic dance. Ravel's "Bolero" is one long crescendo built over a repeated drum rhythm that opens the piece and has an almost hypnotic effect as it is repeated over and over. The melody below, like the rhythm, is repeated over and over but with constantly changing orchestration. Try to name the different instruments you hear playing the melody.

84

Melody in Music

What is a melody? You might say that a melody is a tune you can sing, hum, or whistle. Or, melody is that part of music you can most easily remember. Think of some of your favorite songs. Speak the words. Do the melodies follow the rhythm of the spoken words? Originally, melodies were a way of emphasizing the meaning and mood of the words.

Some of the earliest melodies were sung in connection with religious rituals. Primitive tribes sang chants to their various gods and idols. As new religions emerged, chants became an important part of worship services. The early Christian chant, "Dies Irae," was sung as a part of the religious service for the dead. Look at the words and speak them. Then sing the chant and notice how the melody emphasizes the word inflections.

Dies Irae

GREGORIAN CHANT

Di - es i - rae, di - es il - la, Sol - vet — sae - clum — in fa - vil - la.

A series of scales, called *modes*, evolved from this early church music. The melodies of many folk songs are based on these church modes. One of them, the *Dorian mode*, is used in the familiar folk song, "As I Roved Out."

As I Roved Out

AMERICAN FOLK SONG

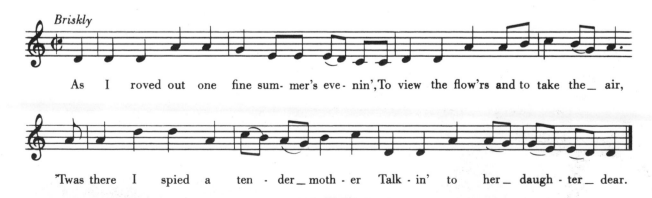

Briskly

As I roved out one fine sum- mer's eve- nin', To view the flow'rs and to take the — air,

'Twas there I spied a ten - der — moth - er Talk - in' to her — daugh - ter — dear.

85

In This Land

FROM ISAIAH 35:1
WORDS ADAPTED BY M. A. DUFAY
MUSIC BY D. ZEHAVI

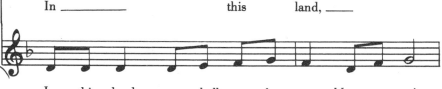

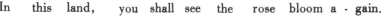

Our major scale corresponds to the *Ionian mode*. Another mode, the *Aeolian*, is used frequently in folk songs.

This mode is the basis of our three minor scales. "In This Land" is a very moving example of a minor-modal melody.

Trust in the Lord, _____

Trust in the Lord, who has made ___ lame men walk,

Blind men see, and the wil - der - ness re - joice.

Trust in the Lord, _____

Trust in the Lord, for this land ___ shall be glad,

In this ___ land.

And its peo - ple blessed with joy and sing - ing.

All melodies consist of an organized series of tones of varying pitch and duration. How many kinds of melodies have you heard? Can you name ways in which a melody progresses from tone to tone? The melody of "In This Land" moved primarily by step. Many songs with a strong rhythmic feeling use repeated tones to accentuate the rhythm. Listen for repeated tones in the first part of "Cindy."

In the second part of "Cindy," there are two syncopated patterns that create a feeling of forward movement, as do these two patterns:

Can you find other rhythm patterns?

Cindy

AMERICAN FOLK SONG

Harmony is often written at the interval of a third or sixth because these intervals are pleasing to our ears.

Rhythmically

CHORUS

Git a-long home, Cin-dy, Cin-dy, Git a-long home, Cin-dy, Cin-dy,

Git a-long home, Cin-dy, Cin-dy, I'll mar-ry you ___ some day. *Fine*

SOLO

1. I wish I was an ap - ple a - hang - in' on a tree,
2. I went to see my Cin - dy, she's stand - in' in the door,
3. My Cin - dy got re - li - gion, she had it once be - fore,

D. C. al Fine

And ev - 'ry time my Cin - dy passed, she'd take a bite of me.
Her shoes and stock - ings in her hand, her feet all over the floor.
And when she hears my ban - jo, she's the first one on the floor.

88

Overture

FROM "THE BARBER OF SEVILLE"
BY GIOACCHINO ROSSINI

Unlike the "Carmen Overture" on page 19, which uses melodies taken from the opera itself, the "Overture to the Barber of Seville" does not give us a preview of the melodies we are to hear later. The overture begins with a light melody made up of ascending, repeated notes marked *andante* (at a moderate speed) and *maestoso* (majestically). The first theme of the main body of the overture has a rather agitated character and is marked *allegro vivace* (very fast).

This melody is followed by trumpet calls built, for the most part, on ascending chordal patterns. These trumpet calls are answered by the woodwinds. Then, following a solo passage for violin, we hear the second theme.

After this gay, frivolous melody is repeated, we hear a characteristic device for which Rossini is famous: a long, sustained crescendo. In his overtures, the indication *crescendo poco a poco* (gradually louder, little by little) is something of a trademark. As you listen, notice the many repetitions of the melody, the progression from soft to very loud and the movement from long notes to shorter values.

Following the exciting *crescendo*, we again hear theme 1 and then theme 2. The famous Rossini *crescendo*, repeated and extended, leads to the conclusion of the overture. What kind of movement do all of these melodies have in common?

Many melodies are made up of skips between chord tones.
Look for chord outlines in "Clementine."

Clementine

AMERICAN FOLK SONG

Verse: In a cav-ern, in a can-yon, Ex-ca-vat - ing for a mine,
Refrain: Oh my dar - ling, oh my dar - ling, Oh my dar - ling Clem-en - tine!

Dwelt a min - er, For-ty Nin - er, And his Daugh-ter Clem-en - tine!
You are lost and gone for-ev - er, Dread-ful sor - ry Clem-en - tine!

In "Mule Skinner Blues," you will also find skips within the
tonic chord (F-A-C), Note, however, that the skips alternate
between a major third (F-A) and a minor third (F-Ab). This
alternation is characteristic of the blues style.

Mule Skinner Blues

AMERICAN FOLK BLUES

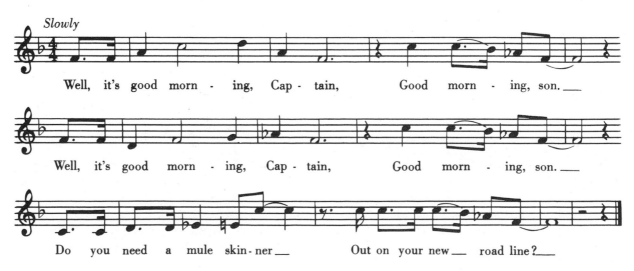

Well, it's good morn - ing, Cap - tain, Good morn - ing, son. __

Well, it's good morn - ing, Cap - tain, Good morn - ing, son. __

Do you need a mule skin-ner __ Out on your new __ road line? __

Most melodies consist of regular phrases. Each phrase comes to a feeling of rest, or *cadence,* before moving on to the next phrase. In most songs, the end of a melodic phrase corresponds to the end of a line of poetry. "Drink to Me Only with Thine Eyes" is a song in which both poetry and melody flow in even, four-measure phrases, with a noticeable pause at the end of each phrase.

Drink to Me Only with Thine Eyes

WORDS BY BEN JONSON
ENGLISH MELODY

The melodies of some songs and many instrumental compositions are made up of long phrases of varied lengths. Listen to Samuel Barber's "Adagio for Strings." Do the cadences occur at regular or irregular time intervals? Notice how smoothly the phrases flow from one to another, like an unending chain.

Cockles and Mussels

IRISH FOLK SONG

In verse three, how has the melody been changed to match the mood of the words?

Allegro moderato

S
A

1. In   Dub - lin's fair   cit - y,   Where girls   are   so   pret - ty,
2. She   was   a   fish - mon - ger, But sure   'twas 'no   won - der,

'Twas   there   I   first   saw   my   sweet   Mol - ly   Ma - lone;
For   so   were her   fa - ther and   moth - er   be - fore;

She   wheeled her wheel - bar - row Through streets broad   and   nar - row,
They   each   wheeled a   bar - row Through streets broad   and   nar - row,

Cry - ing, "Cock - les   and   mus - sels!   A - live,   a - live,   oh!

REFRAIN

A - live,   a - live oh! ___   A - live,   a - live,   oh! ___

Fine

Cry - ing, Cock - les   and   mus - sels!   A - live,   a - live,   oh!"

92

Slower

p

3. She died of a fev - er, And noth - ing could save her,

And that was the end of sweet Mol - ly Ma - lone;

Her ghost wheels her bar - row through streets broad and nar - row,

D. S. al Fine

Cry - ing, "Cock - les and mus - sels! A - live, a - live, oh!"

Loch Lomond

OLD SCOTCH MELODY

In "Loch Lomond," the smooth melodic flow of the verse is contrasted with the more vigorous movement of the refrain. Although the melodic contour is the same, the melodic rhythm has been altered. Where does this occur?

Slowly

VERSE

By — yon bon - nie banks and by yon bon - nie braes, Where the

sun shines bright on Loch Lo - mond; Where me and my true love were

ev - er wont to gae, On the bon - nie, bon - nie banks of Loch Lo - mond.

REFRAIN

Oh, ye'll take the high road, and I'll take the low road, and

I'll be in Scot - land a - fore ye; But me and my true love will

nev - er meet a - gain, On the bon - nie, bon - nie banks of Loch Lo - mond.

The melodies of some folk songs have inspired composers to write an accompaniment that goes beyond the simple chords of most folk songs. In "Sunday," Brahms combined melody, words, and accompaniment in art song style.

Sunday

TRANS. BY GILBERT COOK
UHLAND FOLK MELODY

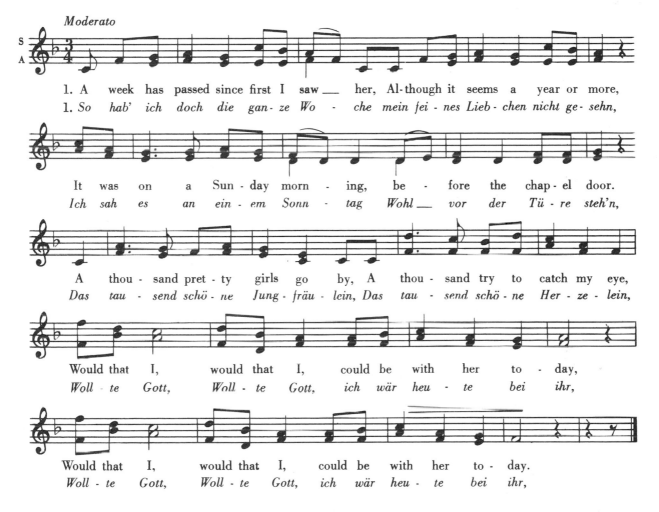

Moderato

1. A week has passed since first I saw her, Al-though it seems a year or more,
1. *So hab' ich doch die gan-ze Wo-che mein fei-nes Lieb-chen nicht ge-sehn,*

It was on a Sun-day morn-ing, be-fore the chap-el door.
Ich sah es an ein-em Sonn-tag Wohl vor der Tü-re steh'n,

A thou-sand pret-ty girls go by, A thou-sand try to catch my eye,
Das tau-send schö-ne Jung-fräu-lein, Das tau-send schö-ne Her-ze-lein,

Would that I, would that I, could be with her to-day,
Woll-te Gott, Woll-te Gott, ich wär heu-te bei ihr,

Would that I, would that I, could be with her to-day.
Woll-te Gott, Woll-te Gott, ich wär heu-te bei ihr,

2. But though a week pass till I see her
I'll gladly wait till then.
For she'll come back to the chapel door,
And I'll see her once again.
A thousand pretty girls go by,
A thousand try to catch my eye,
Would that I, would that I could be with her today,
Would that I, would that I could be with her today!

2. *So will mir doch die ganze Woche*
Das Lachen nicht vergeh'n,
Ich sah es an einem Sonntag
Wohl in die Kirche geh'n:
Das tausend schöne Jungfräulein,
Das tausend schöne Herzelein,
Wollte Gott, wollte Gott, ich wär heute bei ihr,
Wollte Gott, wollte Gott, ich wär heute bei ihr!

Pennies from Heaven

WORDS BY JOHN BURKE
MUSIC BY ARTHUR JOHNSTON

Note the sharp contrast between the A and B sections of this song. Note also, that the second part of the refrain begins like the first part but ends very differently.

Not too fast

A long time a - go; a mil - lion years B. C. _____

The best things in life were ab - so - lute - ly free; _____

But no one _____ ap - pre - ci - at - ed _____ a sky that was al - ways blue;

And no one _____ con - grat - u - lat - ed _____ a moon that was al - ways new. _____

So it was planned that they would van - ish now and then, _____

And you must pay be - fore you get them back a - gain.

That's what storms were made for, And you should - n't be a - fraid, for

Evening Star

FROM TANNHAUSER
WORDS ADAPTED BY A. WILHELMSEN
MUSIC BY RICHARD WAGNER

This aria is from Wagner's opera, "Tannhauser." How would you compare this melody to that of the "Ride of the Valkyries" on page 25?

O ev'n - ing star, ___ so pure ___ and bright, Sad - ly I gaze ___ on
O! du mein hol - der A - bend - stern, wohl grüsst' ich im - mer

you ___ this night. Take from my heart these pains ___ of love, Bear her in
dich ___ so gern; vom Her - zen, das sie nie ___ ver - rieth, grü - sse sie

ra - diance to Heav'n ___ a - bove. Take her be - yond this vale ___ of sor - row,
wenn sie vor - bei ___ dir zieht, wenn sie ent - schwebt dem Thal ___ der Er - den,

To fields of light ___ that know ___ no mor - row; Take her be - yond this
ein sel' - ger En - gel dort ___ zu wer - den, wenn sie ent - schwebt dem

vale ___ of sor - row, To fields of light that ___ know ___ no mor - row.
Thal ___ der Er - den, ein sel' - ger En - gel ___ dort ___ zu wer - den.

Notice the number of accidentals found in this melody. These accidentals create a strong *chromatic* feeling and add a special tonal color to the melody. The accidentals are not used merely as embellishments or decorations but are an important stylistic element. To see just how important the accidentals are, sing the melody without them and listen to how commonplace and flat the music sounds. The Romantic period in general and Wagner in particular used chromaticism to enrich both harmony and melody. Listen carefully for the chromaticism Rimsky-Korsakoff uses in the music of the "Bridal Procession" appearing on the next page.

98

Bridal Procession

FROM "THE GOLDEN COCKEREL"
BY RIMSKY-KORSAKOFF

"Le Coq d'Or," or "The Golden Cockerel," is a "spoof," fantasy opera written by Rimsky-Korsakoff in 1907.

King Didon, the hero, is a very vain king who depends on the Golden Cockerel (a gift from his astrologer) to warn him of danger. In return, King Didon has promised the astrologer anything he wishes. During a battle, King Didon captures a beautiful prisoner, Queen Shemakhan, whom he plans to marry. The music we hear is the "Bridal Procession" as King Didon leads in the queen.

First, we hear the sound of far-off trumpets heralding the procession.

The theme below is a musical description of Queen Shemakhan. It is played softly on the higher-sounding instruments.

In contrast to the "feminine" melody of the queen, King Didon's music is masculine and triumphant.

The procession continues and the music gets louder and louder. The astrologer breaks into the march. He has decided on his wish—to marry the queen. The king is furious and slays him on the spot. The Golden Cockerel, seeing that the astrologer is dead, attacks the king so viciously that he, too, is slain. The music and the procession end abruptly with the death of King Didon.

Tanko Bushi

WORDS BY RON PEXTON
JAPANESE FOLK MELODY

Note the extremely wide range in the melody of "Tanko Bushi" (A♭ to F, an octave and a sixth).

Vigorously

See the full moon ___ shin-ing bright-ly, ___ See the moon ___ in the
Tsu - ki ga ___ *de - ta de - ta,* ___ *Tsu - ki ga* ___ *de -*

sky. ___ Yoi! Yoi! A - bove the moun-tain it has ___ come out to
ta ___ *Yoi! Yoi! Mi - i - ke ta - n - ko* ___ *no u - e*

shine on our dance. While the coal smoke ___ from the chim - ney
ni ___ *de - ta. Am - ma - ri* ___ *en - to - tsu* ___ *ga*

tall curls ___ up ___ to the sky. Mis - ter Moon, Sir, ___ Please ___
ta - ka - i ___ *no - de, Sa - zo - ya* ___ *O Tsuki*

shine through ___ on our dance ___ to - night. Sah no Yoi! Yoi!
sa - n ___ *ke - mu - ta - ka - ro. Sah no Yoi! Yoi!*

Most melodies we sing today use notes from a *diatonic* (seven-note) scale. Some music, particularly that from the Orient, uses a *pentatonic* (five-note) scale. "Tanko Bushi" ("Coalminer's Song") is a popular Japanese folk dance based on a pentatonic scale. It is performed as a circle dance, with everyone singing and acting out the motions of a coalminer as he digs coal, shovels it into his cart, and pushes the cart out of the tunnel.

Playing instruments will add to the performance. On a banjo or violin, pluck the melody with a guitar pick. This will make a sharp, twangy sound similar to the Japanese *shamisen*. With a triangle beater, tap pattern A lightly on a finger cymbal and play pattern B on woodblocks or claves. Play a bass drum on each downbeat and every time the words "Yoi! Yoi!" are sung. In the 9/8 measure, each part adds an extra beat of its pattern.

A. [music notation pattern]

B. [music notation pattern]

In the "Dies Irae" which opened this chapter, the word rhythms and inflections determined the rhythm and the contour of the melody. Here is a contemporary song which also stresses the rhythm of the words, although the rhythm falls into regular metric patterns. In this case, the rhythm is of prime importance and word inflections have less importance in determining melodic contour.

Hawaiian Greeting

WORDS BY FRANCIS ANDERSON
HAWAIIAN MELODY

Smoothly

"A - lo - ha," say is - land - ers, when part - ing or meet - ing, Soft - spok - en

mag - ic, heard as a greet - ing; Hark to the thrill "A - lo - ha" can

send through you, Sing - ing Ha - wai - i's call to you. Here Pa - cif - ic zeph - yrs

rus - tle the palm trees, Fleet - ing ca - ress of a warm breeze, Is - land

blos - soms per - fume the night, Be - neath the south sea moon - light. Is - land

blos - soms per - fume the night, Be - neath the south sea moon - light.

© from "Hawaiian Melodies," by Charles E. King. Used by Permission.

Making Up Melodies

We have heard and sung many different types of melodies in this chapter, and we have discussed various important aspects of each. But perhaps the best way to understand melody is to try to write one of your own.

The "Dies Irae" on page 85 is the first part of a very extended chant.

The Latin text for the third phrase,

Teste Da-vid cum Si-byl-la

closes the first section. Following the free melodic and rhythmic style of the first two phrases, try to set these words to music—then check your solution against the traditional setting printed in your teacher's edition.

Songs in the Dorian mode sound much like songs in the natural minor mode. However, there is a difference caused mainly by the 6th scale degree. This raised 6th scale degree brightens the sound of the melodic line, especially when this tone occurs on strong beats or is stressed in other ways.

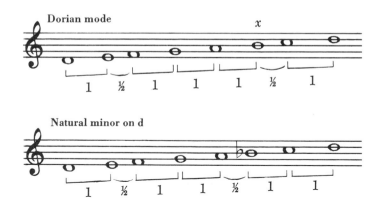

Notice where this 6th scale degree occurs in "As I Roved Out" (page 85) and in the following melodic example. Write words that seem to fit the mood and contour of melody — then experiment with writing your own Dorian melodies.

You will have become familiar with many songs in the minor mode, which occurs naturally on the piano keyboard if you play all the white keys from A to A.

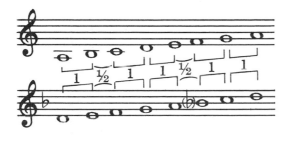

To place the melody of "In This Land" (page 85), in a more singable range, the keynote has been changed to D. A key signature of one flat is needed to maintain the correct pattern of intervals.

Find other minor melodies in this book and think of other well-known minor songs. Then try writing a minor melody of your own. You may find it easier to begin if you first choose words which you feel should be set to a minor melody.

Since all melodies must move either by step, skip, or repeated tones, (or any combination of the three) you can find many examples of each type of melodic movement. However, when writing a melody, you must also consider the rhythm patterns and underlying harmonies which give shape and form to any melody. You may start with a poem, which will help determine the meter and rhythm patterns. Also, the word inflections will suggest a suitable melodic contour. With the simple harmonic frame-work of "Clementine" as a guide, try writing your own melodies of two balanced phrases, using all three types of melodic movement.

$$\text{I} \mid \text{I} \mid \text{I} \mid \text{V}_7 \mid$$
$$\text{V}_7 \mid \text{I} \mid \text{V}_7 \mid \text{I} \mid$$

Limiting the harmony to one chord per measure may help to simplify any problems you might encounter in your first attempts at melody writing. The following tune is an example of the type of melody you could write.

103

Harmony in Music

In many of our daily activities, we must work with other people. If we work well together, we say we are working in harmony. In music, harmony has a specific meaning: two or more tones sounding together. One kind of harmony, *polyphony*, is produced when two or more melodies are sung at the same time.

This Old Hammer

AMERICAN FOLK SONG

Mournfully

1. This old ham-mer _____ killed John Hen-ry, _____
2. This old ham-mer _____ shines like sil-ver, _____

1. This old ham-mer _____ killed John Hen-ry, ___
2. This old ham-mer _____ shines like sil-ver, ___

This old ham-mer _____ killed John Hen-ry, _____
This old ham-mer _____ shines like sil-ver, _____

_____ This old ham-mer _____ killed John Hen-ry, _____
_____ This old ham-mer _____ shines like sil-ver, ___

This old ham-mer _____ killed John Hen-ry, ___ But it
This old ham-mer _____ shines like sil-ver, ___ But it

_____ This old ham-mer _____ killed John Hen-ry, _____
_____ This old ham-mer _____ shines like sil-ver, _____

won't kill me, ___ No, it won't kill me. _____
rings like gold, ___ Yes, it rings like gold. _____

___ But it won't kill me, ___ No, it won't kill me.
___ But it rings like gold, ___ Yes, it rings like gold.

In "This Old Hammer," harmony occurs every time group I sustains the final tone of a phrase and group II echoes the phrase. Add this repeated *ostinato* as another harmony part.

Ostinato

This old ham-mer. ___ This old ham-mer. ___

In a round or canon, we create harmony when two or more groups sing the same melody but each begins singing at a different time. You may also produce harmony by using any phrase of the round as an *ostinato*. Sing the phrase marked *x* as an *ostinato* while another group sings the melody in unison.

Hey, Ho! Nobody Home

Now sing the *ostinato* against the melody performed as a three-part round.

TRADITIONAL ENGLISH ROUND

Gaily

Hey, ho! No-bod-y home, Meat nor drink nor mon-ey have I none,

x

Yet I will be hap - py, Hey, ho! No-bod-y home.

List to the Bells

TRADITIONAL ROUND

Try using the ostinato idea on page 105 with the rounds on this page.

List to the bells, sil-ver-y bells, Rhym-ing and chim-ing, their mel-o-dy swells,

O the bea-ti-ful chim-ing of bells, Bells, bells, chim-ing of bells.

I Love the Mountains

CAMP ROUND

I love the moun-tains and ___ the gold-en hills,

I love the rip-pling brooks and ___ the daf-fo-dils,

I love to live and live to love for all these won-der-ful things. ___

Here is an independent *ostinato* you can sing against the melody of "I Love the Mountains." You might also use it as an introduction to establish the E♭ tonality.

(Repeat 3 times.)

Boom-ta-da-da, boom-ta-da-da, boom-ta-da-da, boom-ta-da-da,

Boom-ta-da-da, boom-ta-da-da, boom-ta-da-boom. ___

A *canon* is similar to a round, but its melody is sung only
once and the voices often, but not always, end together.

The King of Love My Shepherd Is

WORDS BY HENRY W. BAKER
TRADITIONAL IRISH MELODY
SETTING BY CARL SCHALK

Andante

The — King of Love my — Shep - herd is, Whose —

The — King of Love my — Shep - herd

good - ness fail - eth — nev - er; I

is, Whose — good - ness fail - eth — nev -

noth - ing lack if I am His, And

er; I noth - ing lack if I am

He is mine for - ev - er.

His, And He is mine for - ev - er.

107

Maori Love Song

WORDS BY RON PEXTON
MAORI FOLK MELODY

Sometimes a song is written like a canon but the second voice is not an exact duplication of the first. How is the second voice different from the first in this canon from New Zealand?

Moderato

Waves break-ing on the cor - al, White foam and blue
Po - ka - re - ka - re, a - na Nga wai - o Wai -

MELODY

Waves break-ing on the cor - al, White foam and blue wa - ter,
Po - ka - re - ka - re, a - na Nga wai - o Wai - a - pu,

wa - ter, Stir - ring deep with - in my heart, The
a - pu, Whi - ti a - tu ko - e hi - ne,

Stir - ring deep with - in my heart, The long - ing I feel for
Whi - ti a - tu ko - e hi - ne, Ma - ri - no - a - na -

long - ing I feel for you. Oh, my be - lov'd, Come soon to
Ma - ri - no - a na - e. E hi - ne e, Ho - ki - mai

you. Oh, my be - lov'd, Come soon to me.
e. E hi - ne e, Ho - ki - mai ra.

me. Sail o - ver the wa - ters of the trop - ic sea.
ra, Ka - ma te a - u i - te a - ro - ha e.

Sail o - ver the wa - ters of the trop - ic sea.
Ka - ma - te a - u i - te a - ro - ha e.

Another kind of polyphony is produced when two different melodies are heard at the same time. When we sing the melodies of two well-known songs together, we call the combination partner songs. What other partner songs have you sung?

Partner Song

"SAMBALELE"
"SING AND DANCE"

Briskly

Tra la la la la la la la, Tra la la la la la

First we bow po-lite-ly, (po-lite-ly), And then we cir-cle

la la, Tra la la la la la la la,

light-ly, (go light-ly). We keep the rhy-thm spright-ly, (it's spright-ly), And

Tra la la la la la la la,

sing and dance so bright-ly, (so bright-ly). La la la la, la la la la,

Sam-ba-le-le, hear what they're play-ing,
Sam-ba-le-le, rhy-thm to please you,

Lis-ten and do what the mu-sic is say-ing.
Swing-ing and sway-ing and

danc-ing as we do.

La la la la, la la la la la; Tra la la la la.

109

Angela

WORDS BY YVONNE CARR
PORTUGESE FOLK MELODY

Sometimes a second melody is written to be sung with an existing song; we call this a *descant* or *counter-melody*.

An - ge - la, An - ge - la,

1. There's a lit - tle vil - lage near the wind - swept o - cean,
2. Oh, the won - drous joys we knew when love a - wak - ened,
3. As the sun de - scends, my thoughts are ev - er turn - ing,

An - ge - la, An - ge - la,

With a sun - lit path - way lead - ing to the shore.
As we strolled a - long the path - way hand in hand,
To the path - way of my vil - lage by the sea,

An - ge - la, _____

Stroll - ing there, my love and I pledged our de - vo - tion,
Till the storm - toss'd night when my sweet love was tak - en,
And my heart is fill'd with sad - ness and with yearn - ing,

An - ge - la.

Mak - ing vows meant to last for - ev - er - more. _____
Far a - way, far be - yond the shift - ing sand. _____
For the days we stroll'd, just An - ge - la and me. _____

110

In "Streets of Laredo," the five-note counter-melody appears below the main melody. Compare the rhythm and melodic contours of each part.

Streets of Laredo

COWBOY SONG

3. "Get six jolly cowboys to carry my coffin,
   Get six purty maidens to sing me a song;
   Take me to the valley and lay the sod o'er me
   For I'm a young cowboy and know I've done wrong.

4. "Oh, beat the drum slowly and play the fife lowly,
   Play the dead march as you carry me along;
   Put bunches of roses all over my coffin,
   Roses to deaden the clods as they fall."

Rejoice, Beloved Christians

BY JOHANN SEBASTIAN BACH

"Rejoice, Beloved Christians" is an example of instrumental polyphonic writing. Listen to the way the three independent parts combine to create the harmony. The different tone color of each part makes the melodies easy to recognize.

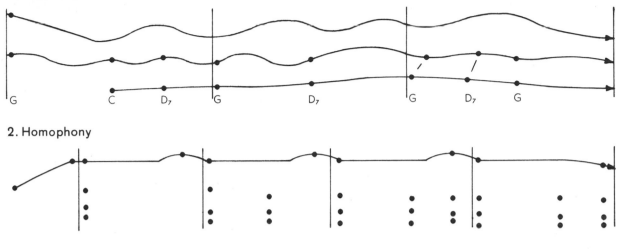

In the "Prelude" by Chopin, we hear how chords add interest to a simple melody. The diagrams show graphically these two approaches to harmony.

Prelude in E minor

BY FRÉDÉRIC CHOPIN

The melody of the following song has not been harmonized for you. The chord changes are indicated. As part of the class sings the melody and your teacher plays the chords, see if you can sing a harmony part on the syllable, "loo."

I Ride an Old Paint

COWBOY SONG

You will have discovered that only two chords are needed to create a suitable harmonization for "I Ride an Old Paint" —the I chord (C chord) and the V_7 chord (G_7 chord). Below are the tones of these chords. Try spacing them differently.

The way you harmonized this song is called "vocal chording."

Jamaican Farewell

WORDS BY M. A. DUFAY
CARIBBEAN FOLK MELODY

Rhythmically

1. Down the bay where the lights were gay, __ I could hear the sing-ing and the
2. Danc-ing girls swing-ing to and fro __ In the mar-ket place where I

mu-sic play, __ And I want-ed to see __ what the fun would be, __ So I
chanced to go, __ And I bought some fish __ that was quite a dish, __ Then I

left my is-land home down Ja-mai-ca way. __ } But sad was I __ to
gave __ it a-way to a gal I know. __ }

REFRAIN

say good-by, __ And I'll be back __ if I swim or fly, __ My heart is down, __

my eyes are turn-ing a-round __ To see my lit-tle girl in Ja-mai-ca town.

3. Though this place is no disgrace,
   I confess the natives are a merry race,
   But I miss my home, no longer want to roam,
   I'll be happy again when I see her face.
   REFRAIN

Here is a vocal chording pattern for "Jamaican Farewell."

Sing on "loo"

(Fare-well Ja-mai-ca, fare-well Ja-mai-ca, fare-well my is-land home.)

To heighten the calypso spirit, sing words instead of "loo."

In the Shade of the Old Apple Tree

WORDS BY HARRY H. WILLIAMS
MUSIC BY EGBERT VAN ALSTYNE

In the blos - soms as you said to me,_____

Said to me,

With a heart that is true, I'll be wait - ing for you,

With a heart that is true, I'll be wait - ing for you,

mp   *rit.*

In the shade of the old ap - ple tree, (ap - ple tree.)

mp   *rit.*

In the shade of the old ap - ple tree, ap - ple tree.

A simple way to harmonize is to sing parallel thirds or sixths.
The songs on the next two pages are harmonized in this way.

117

Shoo, Fly, Don't Bother Me

AMERICAN FOLK SONG

To harmonize this song, you need only the two chords below:

Briskly

MELODY

Shoo, fly, don't both-er me, Shoo, fly, don't both-er me,

Shoo, fly, don't both-er me, For I be-long to some-bod-y. *Fine*

I feel, I feel, I feel, I feel like a morn-ing star;

D. C. al Fine

I feel, I feel, I feel, I feel, I feel like a morn-ing star. So

Fare Thee Well, My Honey

FOLK BLUES

This is an example of *vocal homophony,* two vocal parts supporting the melody.

Slowly

MELODY

mp 1. Oh, some folks say that the blues ain't bad,

Slowly

mp

118

It's the worst old feel - ing that I ev - er had.

Fare thee well, my hon - ey, Fare thee well.

Fare thee well. Fare thee well.

2. If I had wings like Noah's dove,
   I'd fly up the the river to the one I love.
   Fare thee well, my honey,
   Fare thee well.

3. Oh, one of these days, and it won't be long,
   You'll call my name and I'll be gone.
   Fare thee well, my honey,
   Fare thee well.

One of America's most distinctive contributions to music is the "blues;" songs that have grown out of Negro work songs and spirituals. Characteristics of the blues are "blue" notes (see page 90) and texts that tell how the singer has been left alone by an unfaithful loved one.

119

"Heav'n" is a two-part song using a more varied and independent second part. What do you find in the second part that adds
a rich quality and interest to the vocal line?

Heav'n

SPIRITUAL

Notice the use of chromatic notes in the second part.
How do these notes enrich the melody and add to the mood?

I've got a harp, robe, You've got a harp, robe, All God's chil-dren got a harp, robe,
song, song, song,

When I get to heav-en goin' to put on my robe,— Goin' to walk all o - ver God's
play on my harp,— Goin' to play
sing out my song,— Goin' to sing

heav'n,— Heav'n,— heav'n,— Ev-'ry-bod-y talk a-bout

120

heav'n ain't go-in' there, Heav'n, __ heav'n, __ Goin' to play $\left.\begin{array}{c}\text{walk}\\\text{sing}\end{array}\right\}$ all o-ver God's heav'n. __

How would you describe the harmonization of this chorale tune?

O Sacred Head, Now Wounded

TRANS. BY HENRY S. DRINKER
MUSIC BY JOHANN SEBASTIAN BACH

Andante

O sa-cred Head, now wound-ed, With grief and shame weighed down;
Now scorn-ful-ly sur-round-ed With thorns, Thine on-ly crown;

O sa-cred Head, what glo-ry, What bliss till now was Thine!

Yet, though __ de-spised and gor-y, I joy to call Thee mine.

121

Creating Music

Have you ever wondered how a composer writes music?

Writing a musical composition is sometimes like writing a theme for English. One tends to write about something he has done, some place he has been, or something he has seen. Imagination can take you even further than personal experiences. When we create, we begin with an idea. No two people proceed in exactly the same way. Let us investigate some of the ways we might go about creating music.

Let's take a simple American folk tune, "Go Tell Aunt Rhody," and develop it into a longer composition to be both sung and played by a group of instruments.

First, we need an introduction. We can begin with the first two measures of the song with one note changed:

Then make a sequence of these two measures at a higher pitch:

Next, turn the first two measures of the introduction upside down (inversion):

Now add a two measure cadence, and our eight measure introduction is finished:

Here is the complete introduction. Play it and follow it with the tune of "Go Tell Aunt Rhody."

Repeat the tune an octave higher and add a rhythm pattern on tambourine: →

Tap Tap Tap Shake

Repeat the tune once more at a slower tempo and in a different key. A few chords on the Autoharp, piano, or guitar will prepare you for the new key—d minor. Going from one key to another in a piece is called modulation.

G   d min.   A₇   d min.

To make the change of key to d minor even more effective, play "Go Tell Aunt Rhody" in a lower register. All the tones will be below middle C.

For a change in mood and timbre, add a percussion interlude made up of new material. To emphasize the change of mood, play the interlude at a slightly faster tempo.

To complete the composition, combine all of the instruments. A few chords (again played on Autoharp, piano, or guitar) will lead back to the original key of G major.

d min.   a min.   D₇   G

Play the original melody on piano and resonator bells and add a descant on melody bells. The percussion instruments can play their assigned parts. The full closing score appears on the following page, with a four-measure coda.

123

124

Hauling the Nets

CEYLONESE FOLK SONG

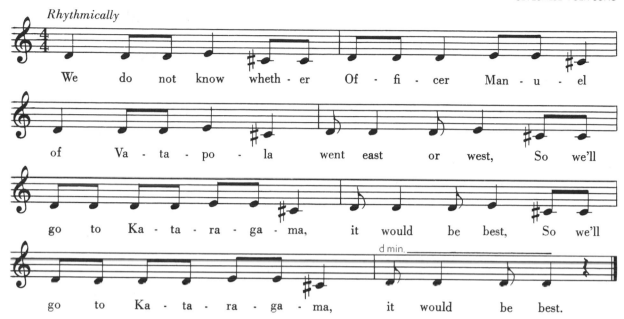

Rhythmically

We do not know wheth - er Of - fi - cer Man - u - el

of Va - ta - po - la went east or west, So we'll

go to Ka - ta - ra - ga - ma, it would be best, So we'll

d min.

go to Ka - ta - ra - ga - ma, it would be best.

The simple melody above should be a challenge to your creativity. It is a folk song from Ceylon that sailors and fishermen often sing to make their working hours pass faster. The sailors pull on their ropes and the fishermen on their nets in rhythm to the melody. How many pulls do you think there would be in each measure? On which beats would they occur?

Make up a rhythm pattern to emphasize the pulling motion. What instruments would be appropriate for this pattern? You might also make up other rhythm patterns derived from the melody—for example, a pattern of steady, repeated eighth notes, or a syncopated pattern based on the rhythm in measures 4 and 6. What other patterns can you create?

You can create harmony by using the vocal chording idea on page 115. At first, use only the d minor (I) and A_7 (V_7) chords. Then add the g minor (IV) chord on the second beat of each measure. The chords may be sung on a neutral syllable, such as "loo," or you might use the words of the song.

Here are the chord tones you will need to use:

When singing with "loo," use this rhythm pattern:

With words, you will, of course, sing the rhythm of the melody. Turn the page to see how you might further develop this song.

You might make up a descant. First, determine how the melody moves. Is it primarily by steps, skips, or repeated notes? Are the note values long or short? Are the rhythm patterns regular, irregular, or syncopated? When you have answered these questions, make up a contrasting descant based on the chord tones you used for the vocal chording. A number of different descants can be made up using only these chord tones. After a little practice, you may want to experiment with passing tones or neighboring tones to add interest and variety.

So far, you have only added to the original melody. Why not extend the piece to make a rondo? (See page 65.) First, you will need to make up a contrasting B section. Since the melody of the first section revolves around only three tones, the melody of the B section might begin by moving boldly up a scale line. How would you complete this melody?

Vocal chording can be used to harmonize your new melody. By *humming* the chord tones, you can add a different timbre.

Use the tune of "Hauling the Nets" for your return to A. For variety, you may want to make up new words, either based on an entirely new idea or a simple variation of the words you have already sung in section A. Now you need eight new measures for the C section. For contrast, you might write a melody using rapid, repeated tones. Try using sixteenth notes. Here is one example:

You could use repeated words, rhythm syllables or nonsense syllables to keep the rhythm of the melody moving. Experiment with different melodies and choose the one you like. When you have finished the C section, repeat A and your rondo is completed—A-B-A-C-A.

Here are five poems of contrasting moods and meters. Try to create songs using these poems for lyrics. First, scan the poems to determine rhythm and meter. Then establish the mood and decide whether a major or minor mode is more suitable.

Block out your harmonies (see page 103) and try to write an appropriate melody. Remember that very few songs are written "all at once." You will probably find that you have to experiment with different ideas before you are satisfied.

THE SOUND OF THE WIND

The wind has such a rainy sound,
Moaning through the town;
The sea has such a windy sound,
Will the ships go down?

The apples in the orchard
Tumble from the tree.
Oh, will the ships go down, go down,
In the windy sea?

—CHRISTINA ROSSETTI

METHUSELAH

Methuselah ate what he found on his plate,
And never, as people do now,
Did he note the amount of the calory count;
He ate it because it was chow.
He wasn't disturbed as at dinner he sat,
Devouring a roast or a pie,
To think it was lacking in granular fat
Or a couple of vitamins shy.
He cheerfully chewed each species of food,
Unmindful of troubles or fears
Lest his health might be hurt
By some fancy dessert;
And he lived over nine hundred years.

—AUTHOR UNKNOWN

THE FLAG GOES BY

Hat's off!
Along the street there comes
A blare of bugles, a ruffle of drums,
A flash of color beneath the sky:
Hats off!
The flag is passing by!

Blue and crimson and white it shines,
Over the steel-tipped, ordered lines.
Hats off!
The colors before us fly;
But more than the flag is passing by.

Hats off!
Along the street there comes
A blare of bugles, a ruffle of drums;
And loyal hearts are beating high:
Hats off!
The flag is passing by!

—HENRY HOLCOMB BENNETT

LIMERICK

There was a young lady of Niger,
Who smiled as she rode on a tiger;
They returned from the ride
With the lady inside,
And the smile on the face of the tiger.

MUSIC OF GROWTH

Music is in all growing things;
And underneath the silken wings
Of smallest insects there is stirred
A pulse of air that must be heard;
Earth's silence lives, and throbs, and sings.

—GEORGE PARSONS LATHROP

Playing Instruments

We all enjoy singing and playing instruments. Instruments may be used to accompany and enrich our singing. Playing instruments can also help us learn many things about music that may be difficult to understand through singing only. How can playing instruments help us know more about rhythm patterns, melody patterns, harmonic structure and mood?

Instruments may be used to suggest a specific land or culture. Percussion instruments have been used in unique ways by people in different countries. In the West Indies, conga drums, bongo drums, maracas, guiros, claves and the casaba are used for characteristic calypso color. Other Latin American countries add tambourines and castanets for a slightly different color. For music of the East, characteristic instruments are temple blocks, finger cymbals, drums and gong.

The Purple Bamboo

WORDS BY IRENE GLASS
CHINESE FOLK SONG

From "Folk Songs from China," collected by Tz-Zeung Koo.
Used by permission of J. Curwen & Sons, Ltd., London.

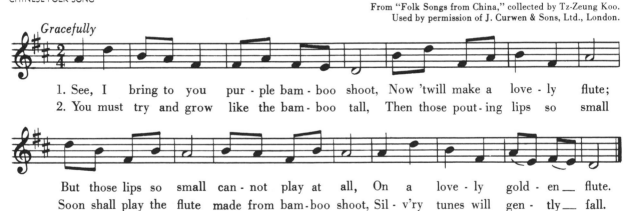

1. See, I bring to you pur-ple bam-boo shoot, Now 'twill make a love-ly flute;
2. You must try and grow like the bam-boo tall, Then those pout-ing lips so small

But those lips so small can-not play at all, On a love-ly gold-en flute.
Soon shall play the flute made from bam-boo shoot, Sil-v'ry tunes will gen-tly fall.

This song uses the tones of a pentatonic scale—D, E, F#, A and B. Using these five tones, create a counter-melody for flute, recorder, or resonator bells to be played as the class sings. An interesting instrumental combination results if the flute plays the written melody as the bells play an improvised part.

The tones will sound well together. Try playing the song as a canon for two flutes with the second player starting after a one measure interval.

Add rhythm instruments to enhance the oriental atmosphere. Here are some patterns you may try.

128

Just as we associate the guitar with Spanish songs, so we think of the ukulele for accompanying Hawaiian songs. Below is the ukulele tablature for some of the most common major and minor keys. What rhythm pattern would you strum?

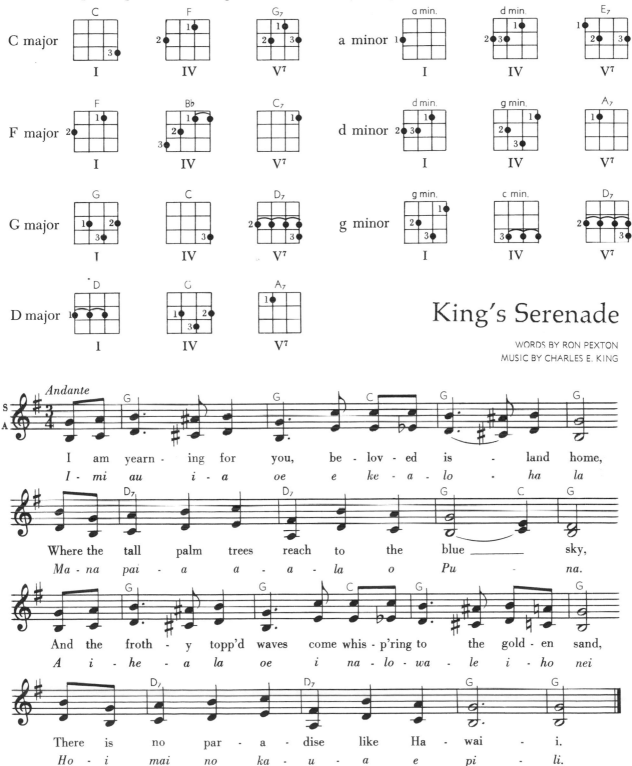

King's Serenade

WORDS BY RON PEXTON
MUSIC BY CHARLES E. KING

Andante

I am yearn - ing for you, be - lov - ed is - land home,
I - mi au i - a oe e ke - a - lo - ha la

Where the tall palm trees reach to the blue _____ sky,
Ma - na pai - a a - a - la o Pu - na.

And the froth - y topp'd waves come whis - p'ring to the gold - en sand,
A i - he - a la oe i na - lo - wa - le i - ho nei

There is no par - a - dise like Ha - wai - i.
Ho - i mai no ka - u - a e pi - li.

A guitar is usually used to accompany songs of Spain and Spanish-speaking countries. On page 132, you will find guitar tablature for the chords needed to accompany "Adios Muchachos." An easy strumming pattern for this song and many songs in 2/4 meter is:

Adios Muchachos

ENGLISH WORDS BY M. A. DUFAY
ARGENTINE FOLK MELODY

Slow tango

A - dios mu - cha - chos, it's with sad - ness I am go - ing,
A - diós mu - cha - chos com - pa - ñe - ros de mi vi - da,

No use pre - tend - ing, this is the end - ing.
Ba - rra que - ri - da de a - que - llos tiem - pos

For all the gay and care - free days we have been know - ing,
Me to - ca a mí hoy em - pren - der la re - ti - ra - da,

A grate - ful heart and hap - py smile we should be show - ing.
De - bo a - le - jar - me de mi bue - na mu - cha - cha - da,

Good - by to you, my friends, a - dios is what I'm say - ing.
A - diós, mu - cha - chos, ya me voy y me re - sig - no

It's time we part - ed, I'm bro - ken - heart - ed,
Con - tra el des - ti - no na - die la ta - lla,

But know mu - cha - chos, des - ti - ny I am o - bey - ing,
Se ter - mi - na - ron pa - ra mí to - das las ja - rras,

130

We'll say *a - dios,* and I'll be on my way.
Mi cuer - po en - fer - mo no re - sis - te más.

No life would I be trad - ing for days of mas - quer - ad - ing,
Dos la - gri - mas sin - ce - ras de - rra mo en mi par - ti - da

And nights of ser - e - nad - ing with voic - es raised on high,
Por la ba - rra que - ri - da que nun - ca me ol - vi - dó

Fare - well to se - nor - it - as we knew, Sal - ud - das
Y al dar - le a mis a - mi - gos mi a - diós pos - tre - ro

To you, And now, a - mi - gos, I say good - by.
Le doy con to - du el al - ma mi ben - di - ción.

Below are three rhythm patterns that may be played as *osti-natos* throughout "Adios Muchachos." Certain instruments are suggested for your use, but you might try switching them from pattern to pattern or even use different instruments appropriate to the song, such as claves and guiros.

Castanets

Drum

Tambourine

The guitar is the most commonly used instrument for accompanying folk songs. It is a more complex instrument than the ukulele and has six strings, tuned E, A, D, G, B, E. Below are the primary chords for several major and minor keys.

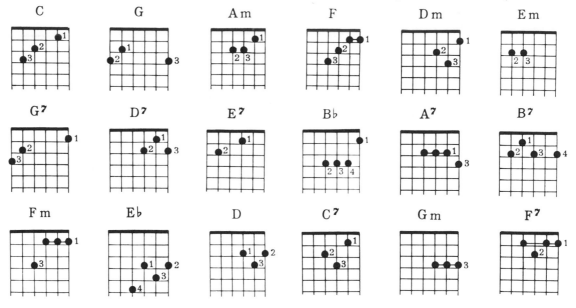

Tzena, Tzena

WORDS BY MITCHELL PARISH
MUSIC BY I. MIRON AND J. GROSSMAN

Lively

Tze - na, Tze - na, Tze - na, Tze - na, How can an - y - thing be plain - er than __ my love for you? __ Tze - na, Tze - na, Tze - na, Tze - na, Don't you know your eyes con - tain a look __ that thrills me thru? __ Tze - na, Tze - na, ev' - ry - one is wait - ing, For a wed - ding they're an -

132

ti - ci - pat - ing, Ev - 'ry - one is hap - py cel - e - brat - ing, Peo - ple

danc - ing in the streets! ___ Clap your hands and raise your voic - es high - er,

Make a cir - cle while we dance a - round the fire ___ Dance the Ho - ra

to your heart's de - sire ___ All the world's in love with Tze - na, Tze - na.

You will find the guitar tablature needed to accompany this song on page 132. Here is a strumming pattern suitable for many songs in 6/8 meter:

Galloping Randy Dandy O

CHANTEY

Gaily

1. Now we're warp - ing her in - to the docks, Way - aye, roll and go! Where the
2. Heave and pull ___ and heave a - way, Way - aye, roll and go! The ___

pret - ty young girls ___ come down in flocks, My gal - lop - ing Ran - dy Dan - dy O!
an - chor's a - board and the cables are stowed, My gal - lop - ing Ran - dy Dan - dy O!

Allegro Moderato

FROM "VIOLIN CONCERTO IN D, OP. 35"
BY PETER TCHAIKOVSKY

Although Tchaikovsky's "Violin Concerto" was not well received by the critics when first performed, its brilliant violin part and flowing melodies quickly established the work as a popular favorite with audiences everywhere.

The first movement opens with a brief orchestral introduction based on the rhythmic pattern found in the first measure of the opening theme. The violin enters and we hear the first theme. Notice how the rhythmic pattern in the last measure is used to lead the solo violin into a repetition of the opening theme in a higher octave.

A short section follows based on the theme below. Note how the rhythm pattern gives a questioning quality to the melody.

A brilliant display passage for the solo violin leads to the second main theme. How does it contrast with the first theme?

In what ways is it similar? The rest of the movement is made up of these themes. Try to identify them as you listen.

134

In "Dark Eyes" (page 5), you have heard how a violin solo can enhance the mood of a sad, mournful song. Why do you think a violin was chosen to accompany this gay, cheerful song? For an example of the violin used as a brilliant solo instrument against a full orchestra, see page 134.

Tom Bolynn

SCOTCH BALLAD

1. Tom Bo-lynn was a Scotch-man born, his shoes worn out, his stock-ings torn;
2. Tom Bo-lynn had no pants to wear, he bought sheep-skin to make a pair;
3. To him his moth-er said one day, "You'll have to go else-where to stay;

His shirt was rag-ged his Spen-cer thin; "'Tis my best suit," said Tom Bo-lynn.
The flesh side out and the hair side in; "They're charm-in' cool," said Tom Bo-lynn.
I can't lie wake and hear you snore, you can't stay in my house no more."

REFRAIN

Tom Bo-lynn, Tom Bo-lynn, Tom Bo-lynn, Hi-ho!

4. Tom got into a hollow tree
   And mos' contented seemed to be.
   The wind did blow and the rain beat in,
   " 'Tis home, sweet home," said Tom Bolynn.

REFRAIN

The Contented Camel

WORDS BY DAVID STEVENS
MUSIC BY FRANCIS AMES

Besides enhancing mood, instruments can be used for descriptive purposes. What does the clarinet add to the humor of this song. What does it describe?

1. Oh, far a - way in E - gypt land A cam - el dwelt con - tent - ed;
2. "It's dry of course, of rain there's none, You nev - er see a street wet;
3. "There is - n't much so - ci - e - ty, The place is un - fre - quent - ed;

He did - n't mind the des - ert sand That stretched for miles on ev - 'ry hand,
But I have yet to see the fun In clouds that hide the ge - nial sun,
But that is all the same to me, From so - cial du - ties I am free,

"Be - cause," said he, "I un - der-stand It can - not be pre - vent - ed."
And as for rain, well I for one, Don't like to get my feet wet!"
And while I have my health," said he, "I'm bound to be con - tent - ed!"

From the "Youth's Companion."

Voices may be substituted for the instrumental parts, singing
"loo" to simulate the sound of flutes. A finger cymbal may be
played on the last note of each phrase.

Lullaby

WORDS BY CHRISTINA ROSSETTI
MUSIC BY ANN MCDONALD DIERS

Stars and Stripes Forever

BY JOHN PHILIP SOUSA

The melodies of this march are simple but stirring.
Can you find where the famous third theme appears
in this excerpt from the full score? (See page 171).

139

Making Up Bell Accompaniments

You have played rhythm patterns on percussion instruments and harmonic accompaniments on string instruments (Autoharp, piano, ukulele). Another element of music, melody, can be played easily on instruments of the bell family; such as song bells, orchestra bells, glockenspiel, and resonator bells.

Let us group the song bells, orchestra bells and glockenspiel together and consider various ways you might use them.

1. by playing the melody in unison as the class sings it.

2. by playing the harmony part (second voice part, *ostinato*, descant, etc.) while the class sings the melody.

3. by playing the melody while the class sings the harmony.

4. by playing a specific melody pattern each time it occurs.

5. by playing a simple harmonic accompaniment to a song, using one mallet in each hand to play two tones of the chords.

The ideas above may be adapted to other mallet instruments such as xylophone and marimba. You will notice that all the instruments of the bell family produce a ringing tone because the bars are made of metal. The timbres of the xylophone and marimba are quite different because the bars are made of wood.

Resonator bells may also be used for any of the activities listed above. Because the resonator bells may be arranged in any order, you can easily isolate scale tones and build different types of scales: major, minor, modal, pentatonic, and whole tone. After you have built a scale, create your own melody.

Resonator bells are also excellent for building chords and playing a harmonic accompaniment. You may do this by having individual players sound the tones of the three primary chords —I, IV, and V_7. For example, in the key of C:

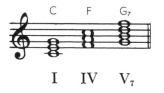

I   IV   V₇

Another easy way to play accompaniments on resonator bells is by placing the bells that form a chord on a desk, table, or in a chord tray. Each chord may be played as a block chord by using a multiple mallet, or the chords may be played in "oom-pah" style by using a single mallet in the left hand and a triple mallet in the right hand. To add variety, the chord tones may be played one after the other as a broken chord. Here are some examples you might use.

Try making up a bell accompaniment for "Michael, Row the Boat Ashore."

Michael, Row the Boat Ashore

TRADITIONAL

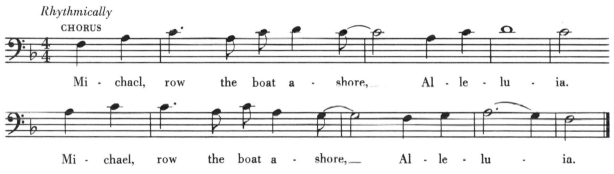

Verse (same melody as chorus):
1. Michael's boat's a music boat, Alleluia,
   Michael's boat's a music boat, Alleluia.
   CHORUS
2. Michael's boat's a gospel boat, Alleluia,
   Michael's boat's a gospel boat, Alleluia.
   CHORUS
3. Gabriel, blow the trumpet horn, Alleluia,
   Blow the trumpet loud and long, Alleluia.
   CHORUS

Many of the songs in your book are suitable for bell accompaniment, After you have had a chance to use the patterns above, make up your own accompaniments using different rhythms.

Reading Music

Learning to read is almost a necessity of life. Unless you can read, life is barren of one of its most delightful pleasures. Think of what you would miss if you had not learned to read words.

Reading music is much the same. To enjoy music to its fullest, you should be able to read it. Then you can learn a song much more easily and not have to depend upon imitating someone else.

The symbols for reading words are an alphabet of 26 letters. The symbols for reading music are notes. Seven letters from the alphabet—A, B, C, D, E, F, G—are used to identify these notes. They are repeated many times, forming octaves as shown by the four octaves on this grand staff.

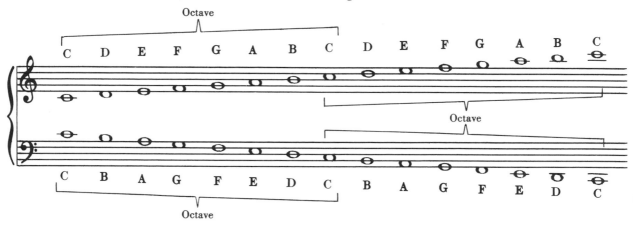

A grand staff of music is called a score. To be able to read music, you must understand the symbols placed on a score. The symbols are a visual representation of how the music should sound. Let us review them in this old college song. Study the symbols and keep their meaning in mind as you sing.

Tell Me Why

COLLEGE SONG

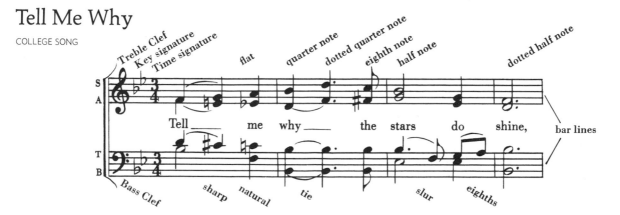

142

When you understand the meaning of the music symbols in this song, you are ready to try reading music at sight. If you are unsure of any symbols, review them with your teacher.

One difficulty in reading music at sight is the problem of keeping time and singing the proper rhythms. Probably the best way to overcome this is to practice rhythm exercises.

In the exercises on the following page, the time signatures used are 2/4, 3/4, and 4/4, because they are the ones you will find most often in the music you sing and play. Beat a steady two, three, or four with your foot (depending on the meter signature) and clap the rhythms of the exercise. Repeat each exercise, beating the meter lightly with your foot and chanting the rhythm on the neutral syllable, "ta."

2/4 time means 2 beats to a measure and a ♩ gets 1 beat

3/4 time means 3 beats to a measure and a ♩ gets 1 beat.

4/4 time means 4 beats to a measure and a ♩ gets 1 beat.

Often indicated by C and called *common time*.

144

Another problem is being able to sing correct pitches. Melodies consist of repeated notes, steps, and skips. You can find examples of each in the melody below. First clap the melodic rhythm and then see if you can read the melody at sight, using letter names, or you might use *do, re, mi* syllables or numbers. Use the symbol you have used in the past. After you have done this, sing the song with words.

The Fountain

WORDS BY MADELEINE A. DUFAY
FRENCH MELODY

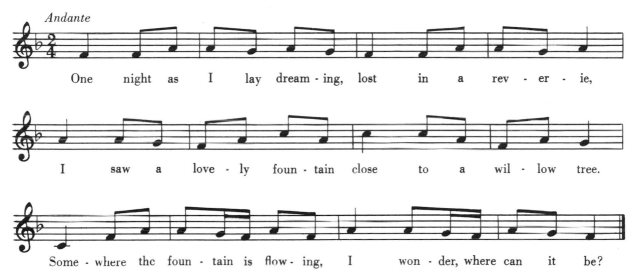

Andante

One night as I lay dream - ing, lost in a rev - er - ie,

I saw a love - ly foun - tain close to a wil - low tree.

Some - where the foun - tain is flow - ing, I won - der, where can it be?

Before singing the review melodies on the next pages, you will need to know the key and the key note.

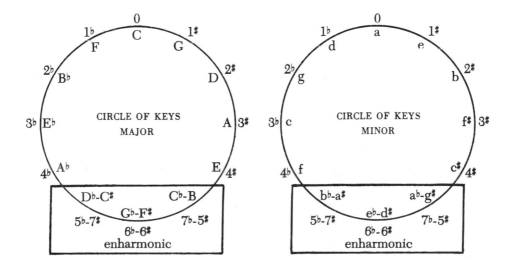

You have learned that mode (whether major or minor) is determined by the pattern of whole- and half-steps.

A major scale has half-steps between 3—4 and 7—8. Below is a picture of a *C major scale* showing notes on the staff and piano keys that match the notes.

A minor scale has half-steps between 2—3 and 5—6. Below is a picture of an *a minor scale* with the notes on the staff and piano keys that match the notes.

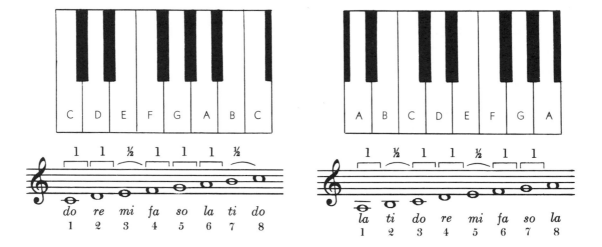

Using the patterns above, construct major scales on E and A♭ and minor scales on d and e. You will have to use accidentals to attain the correct order of intervals. When the scale is complete, place the accidentals at the beginning of the staff following the clef sign. This becomes the key signature.

To find the keynote in a major key with sharps in the signature, remember that the sharp farthest to the right is *ti* or 7. To find *do* or 1, simply count up one half-step to the keynote.

To find the keynote in a major key with flats in the signature, remember that the flat farthest to the right in the key signature is *fa* or 4. To find *do* or 1, count down 4 tones.

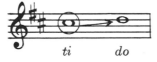

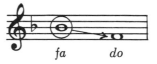

To find the keynote in a minor key with sharps in the signature, remember that the sharp farthest to the right is *ti* or 2. To find *la* or 1, count down 1 whole-step.

To find the keynote in a minor key with flats in the signature, remember that the flat farthest to the right, is *fa* or 6. To find *la* or 1, count up 3 tones.

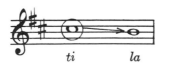

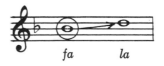

Identify the key and locate the keynote.
Notice the scale patterns in the song.

O Give Thanks
FRENCH ROUND

After you have determined the key, find
two phrases that are exactly alike. By rec-
ognizing like phrases, you will be able to
read more quickly and easily.

We Thank Thee
BY LOWELL MASON

The following melody is from a horn sextet by Mozart. It
contains many repeated notes and scale passages. The accent
marks indicate a slight stress on the notes they mark. Sing the
melody on "ta" to add rhythmic bite.

Theme
FROM "A MUSICAL JOKE"
BY W. A. MOZART

147

The Mozart variations on page 62 use a familiar theme in the key of C major. Here are the first 8 measures. The opening skip is from *do* to *so*, tones of the I chord. The rest of the melody is stepwise, descending by scale tones to *do*.

Sing the same melody in the key of c minor.

When you sang this tune in c minor, you lowered the third and sixth tones of the major scale—causing half-steps between 2-3 and 5-6. All scales based upon the same keynote have the same basic tonality, but mode (major or minor) is determined chiefly by the third scale degree. The lowered third scale degree gives a minor scale its distinctive quality.

Do-mi-so or 1-3-5 are the most important tones in the construction of a scale. When sounded together, they form the tonic chord—the I chord. In this chord, *do* (1) is important as the keynote or tonal center; *mi* (3) is important for the tonal color (major or minor) that it gives to a scale or chord; while *so* (5) provides a feeling of stability, and the interval 1←→5 outlines the chord.

Here is the I chord in C major: Here is the I chord in c minor:

Which tone is different? Again, notice that the third scale degree is a variable "color" tone that establishes the mode.

Here is a familiar melody for you to recognize from just the notation. What is its name? There are many skips of tones within the major I chord. In measure 7, the skips outline another very important chord, the V chord. (C-E-G).

Here is part of a minor melody which some of you may recognize at sight. The I chord is outlined by the three opening notes. Can you identify the key from these three notes? Find another place where the melody outlines the I chord.

The examples in this section have covered many of the problems you encounter in reading music. Apply the techniques you have learned in reading songs throughout the book.

Drama and Music

Can you imagine a movie or television program without music? Music is used to create a mood, help underline the dramatic action, and help tell the story. Drama and music have been combined in many different ways; opera, ballet, operetta, musicals, and incidental music.

There is a great deal of background music that contributes to the overall mood. There are some movies that go further and feature songs that become popular favorites. In the movie, "The Bells of St. Mary," Bing Crosby, playing a priest, sang this song to a group of orphans.

Aren't You Glad You're You?

FROM "THE BELLS OF ST. MARY'S"
WORDS BY JOHNNY BURKE
MUSIC BY JIMMY VAN HEUSEN

Liltingly

Ev - 'ry time you're near a rose, Aren't you glad you've got a nose?

And if the dawn is fresh with dew, Aren't you glad you're you?

When a mead - ow lark ap - pears, Aren't you glad you've got two ears?

And if your heart is sing - ing, too, Aren't you glad you're you?

You can see a sum - mer sky Or touch a friend - ly hand

150

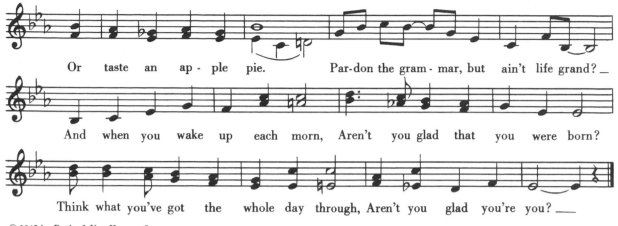

Or taste an ap-ple pie. Par-don the gram-mar, but ain't life grand? ___

And when you wake up each morn, Aren't you glad that you were born?

Think what you've got the whole day through, Aren't you glad you're you? ___

A unique contribution to music for the theatre is the contemporary Broadway musical. Our current musicals are an outgrowth of the early operettas of Romberg, Friml, and Herbert. "Some Day" is a typical love song from a romantic operetta. It is sung by the hero and the leading lady.

Some Day

FROM "THE VAGABOND KING"
WORDS BY BRIAN HOOKER
MUSIC BY RUDOLF FRIML

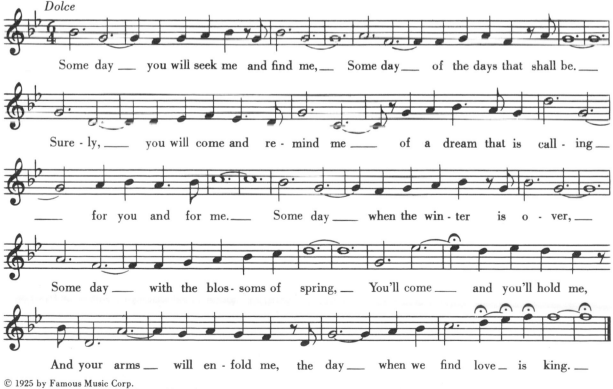

Some day ___ you will seek me and find me, ___ Some day ___ of the days that shall be. ___

Sure - ly, ___ you will come and re - mind me ___ of a dream that is call - ing ___

___ for you and for me. ___ Some day ___ when the win - ter is o - ver, ___

Some day ___ with the blos - soms of spring, ___ You'll come ___ and you'll hold me,

And your arms ___ will en - fold me, the day ___ when we find love ___ is king. ___

151

Music from Tin Pan Alley

The greatest single influence in determining the style or idiom of popular music came from "Tin Pan Alley." This street of song, which began in Union Square in New York City, moved its quarters in the early 1900s to 28th Street. There, composers of dance music, hit writers of every race and nationality came to sell or buy the music America wanted to hear. The name, "Tin Pan Alley," was given to it by a journalist who was preparing an article on popular music for a newspaper. While at one of the offices gathering material for his article, he heard an upright piano in which someone had stuffed strips of paper through the piano strings to produce a tinny effect. These sounds gave the journalist the title for his article, *Tin Pan Alley*. From the time his piece was published, 28th Street and the American popular music industry has been known as Tin Pan Alley.[1]

Among the leading writers of ballads in Tin Pan Alley in the early 1900's was Harry Von Tilzer who wrote the old favorites, "Wait Till the Sun Shines, Nellie" and "I Want a Girl Just Like the Girl Who Married Dear Old Dad."

In the second decade of the 1900's, three composers who began their careers in the Alley brought some of the melody, rhythm and harmony of classical music to popular music. The music of Jerome Kern, Irving Berlin and George Gershwin is as stimulating today as it was then.

Jerome Kern's association with the Alley began in 1905. He had studied at the New York College of Music but his schooling was interrupted by a brief and unprofitable stint in his father's merchandising business. His enthusiasm for music led him to 28th Street where he worked as a song plugger, playing for performers and entertainers and trying to sell the latest publications. After this apprenticeship, he began writing his own tunes and in 1914 had his first outstanding Broadway success with the musical, *The Girl from Utah*, with the unforgettable song, "They Didn't Believe Me." "Look for the Silver Lining" was introduced in the show *Sally* and later he wrote *Show Boat* which had a tremendous impact.

Like Kern, Irving Berlin had his first experiences in Tin Pan Alley but, unlike Kern, he had no musical training. He started as a lyricist but decided he could write tunes as well, as was proved by "Alexander's Ragtime Band." Songwriters were beginning to concentrate on the vigorous rhythms and accents of ragtime rather than on the more formal, evenly balanced melodies and rhythms of past popularity. Though the style was not entirely new to Tin Pan Alley, Berlin invested it with new vitality and freshness. A personal tragedy caused Berlin to return to the writing of sentimental ballads and some of his most beautiful love songs, "What'll I Do?" and "All Alone," were written in this period. "Always" and "Remember" were expressions of his love for Ellin Mackay. After a difficult courtship, they were married and the years that followed brought the enduring "Easter Parade" and "White Christmas."

[1] David Ewen, *American Popular Music* p. 165.

One of the composers most strongly influenced and inspired by Berlin was George Gershwin. A piano teacher recognized the boy's early talents and encouraged him to study harmony and theory. He found a place as staff pianist in Tin Pan Alley and came in direct contact with the best popular tunes of the day. Soon he was writing songs for Broadway revues. "Swanee," written for a stage production and introduced by Al Jolson, became an instant hit. Gershwin's brother, Ira, provided him with lyrics for a number of musical comedies. Among them were *Lady, Be Good!* from which came the exciting, "Fascinating Rhythm." Up to 1930, the Gershwins were represented on Broadway by half a dozen musicals which featured such songs as "Someone to Watch Over Me," " 'S Wonderful," "Embraceable You," "But Not For Me," and "Bidin' My Time." The songs Gershwin wrote for these musicals played a large part in making jazz a sophisticated art. Ferde Grofe, the composer of *Grand Canyon Suite,* also wrote excellent symphonic jazz scores for Paul Whiteman, the popular "King of Jazz." These three outstanding exponents of symphonic jazz teamed up for a single effort and produced "Rhapsody in Blue." This work was by no means the first piece of serious music to use popular American idioms. Before the "Rhapsody," there were works like Debussy's "Golliwog's Cakewalk," Satie's "Parade," and Stravinsky's "Ragtime." Each of these incorporated in larger classical forms the techniques and styles of American popular music. But none of these works had the impact on the music world of "Rhapsody in Blue." It brought complete acceptance of American popular music among most serious musicians. Gershwin's last serious work is considered his greatest —the opera, "Porgy and Bess," written in the year 1935.

The names of Cole Porter, Rodgers and Hart, Noel Coward, and Vincent Youmans, are among those whose music filled the theatres in the years between 1920 and 1950. From the musical plays they wrote came songs like "Tea for Two," "I'll See You Again," "You Do Something to Me," and others too numerous to mention.

A song destined to become one of the all-time classics did not come out of Tin Pan Alley, nor was it a "show" tune. This was "Star Dust," written by Hoagy Carmichael, a lawyer from Bloomington, Indiana. After "Star Dust," Carmichael gave up his practice and went on to write music for the movies. He was soon offered featured roles in motion pictures, on radio and television.

The popular song which had been so successful in Union Square and in Tin Pan Alley was finding another home. When sound came to the screen and talking pictures needed more and more songs, motion picture producers bought rights to Broadway musicals and purchased some of New York's important song-publishing firms, thus providing Hollywood with a large and handy supply of music to draw on. For the first time, popular songs written directly for the movies rivaled in popularity those for the stage. The songwriting team of De Sylva, Brown and Henderson wrote for these celebrated musicals of early talking pictures—*The Singing Fool,* and *Sunny Side Up.* Later, the immortal "Over the Rainbow" was written by Harold Arlen for *The Wizard of Oz.* With Johnny Burke as lyricist, Jimmy Van Heusen wrote many songs for films including "Swinging on a Star," from *Going My Way* and "Aren't You Glad You're You," from *The Bells of St. Mary.* The era of Tin Pan Alley had come to a close.

Seventy-six Trombones

FROM "THE MUSIC MAN"
WORDS AND MUSIC
BY MEREDITH WILLSON

"The Music Man," a recent Broadway musical, is based on the development of school and community bands in our country. Harold Hill, the "music man," is a traveling musical instrument salesman who organizes a boys band in River City, Iowa. "Seventy-six Trombones" is one of the most popular songs from this score.

Sev - en - ty six trom - bones led the big pa - rade, __ With a hun - dred and
Sev - en - ty six trom - bones led the big pa - rade, __ When the or - der to

ten cor - nets close at hand. ___ They were fol - lowed by rows and rows of the
march rang out loud and clear. ___ Start - ing off with a big bang - bong on a

fin - est vir - tu - o - sos, The cream of ev - 'ry fa - mous band. ___
Chi - nese gong, By a big bang - bong - er at the rear. ___

Sev - en - ty six trom - bones caught the morn - ing sun, ___ With a hun - dred and
Sev - en - ty six trom - bones hit the coun - ter point, ___ While a hun - dred and

154

ten cor - nets right be - hind._____ There were more than a thou - sand reeds spring-ing
ten cor - nets played the air._____ Then I mod - est - ly took my place as the

up   like   weeds, There were horns of   ev - 'ry shape and kind. __
one   and on - ly bass, And I   oom - pahed up   and down the square. __

There were cop - per bot - tom tim - pa - ni in horse pla - toons, __   Thun - der - ing,

thun - der - ing, all   a - long the way.   Dou - ble bell eu - pho - ni - ums   and

big bas - soons, _____   Each bas - soon ___ hav - ing his big fat say.

155

There were fif-ty mount-ed can-non in the bat-ter-y, _____ Thun-der-ing,

thun-der-ing, loud-er than be-fore. Clar-i-nets of ev-'ry size and

D. S. al Fine

trum-pet-ers who'd im-pro-vise a full oc-tave high-er than the score.

Connais-tu le Pays?

FROM "MIGNON"
TRANS. BY M. A. DUFAY
MUSIC BY AMBROISE THOMAS

Operettas and musicals include spoken dialogue and songs, while in opera, all the words are sung. In this aria, Mignon sings of her homeland, from which she was abducted as a child.

Andante

Do ___ you know that ___ fair land where the orange blos-soms bloom, ___
Con - nais-tu le ___ pa-ys où fleu-rit l'o-ran-ger, ___

Gold-en mead-ows, I see, _____ and the red ro-ses grow-ing,
Le ___ pa-ys des fruits d'or _____ et des ro-ses ver-meil-les?

Where — the gay songs — of birds — are the sweet-est to me, —
Où — la bri - se est — plus dou - ce, et l'oi-seau plus lé - ger, —

And the soft air is filled — with breez-es gen-tly blow-ing,
Où dans tou-te sai-son — bu-ti-nent les a-beil-les,

Where the sun warm-ly shines, Bring-ing the dawn a-new, Wak-ing a love-ly morn
Où ray-on-ne et sou-rit, comme un bien-fait de Dieu, Un é-ter-nel prin-temps

to a sky ev-er blue? — A-las! — could I once more be-hold it,
sous un ciel tou-jours bleu? — He-las! — que ne puis-je te sui-vre

Or do I seek in vain, will I find it a-gain? It's there, —
Vers ce ri-vage heu-reux, d'où le sort m'e-xi-la! C'est là, —

It's there, the place where I long to be, to love, to live there for-ev-er,
C'est là que je vou-drais vi-vre, ai-mer, ai-mer et mou-rir! —

My land, the home-land so dear to me, It's there, ah! — it's there!
C'est là que je vou-drais vi-vre, c'est là! oui, — C'est là!

Notice how the accidental, B♭, alters the melody at
the word, "Alas," and intensifies the nostalgic mood.

La Donna è Mobile

FROM "RIGOLETTO"
TRANS. BY H. G. TREBILCOX
MUSIC BY GUISEPPE VERDI

This lively melody is one of the most familiar tenor arias in all opera. The lyrics express the Duke of Mantua's cynical attitude toward all women.

Allegretto

Wom - an is like a breeze, Flit - ting a - mong the trees, Oh, what a spell she weaves,
La don - na è mo - bi - le qual piu - ma al ven - to, mu - ta d'ac - cen - to

Not car - ing whom she grieves. She may be full of grace, Have such a ten - der face,
e di pen - sie - ro. Sem - pre un a - ma - bi - le leg - gia - dro vi - so,

She'll lead a mer - ry chase, But you can't win the race. Can't live with - out her,
in pian - to o in ri - so, è men - zo - gne - ro. La don - na è mo - bil

You're mad a - bout her, Though you may doubt her, You can't re - sist.
qual piu - ma al ven - to, mu - ta d'ac - cen - to e di pen - sier,

You can't re - sist.
e di pen - sier,

Ah, _____

et, _____

You can't re - sist.
e di pen - sier.

Swan Lake

BY PETER TCHAIKOVSKY

"Swan Lake" was the first of Tchaikovsky's three ballets. While the others ("Sleeping Beauty" and "The Nutcracker") were quickly accepted by the public and the critics, "Swan Lake" was not a success at its first performance in 1877, because it was badly danced and Tchaikovsky's music had been altered and cut by the theatre director. When the ballet was revived in 1895 with the music played as it was originally written, it very quickly became a popular favorite.

The story of "Swan Lake" is too involved to explain in detail. Briefly, it concerns a queen and her ladies who have been changed into swans by an evil magician. Only for a brief time each night can the swans return to their human forms. It is during this time that the Swan Queen meets and falls in love with Prince Siegfried. After a series of misunderstandings and adventures, the magic spell is broken and the queen and her ladies are free forever.

The entire ballet takes a full evening to perform. It is customary to present only Act II as part of a program containing other ballets. In Act II, the Prince is hunting with his men when they see a swan wearing a crown. The swan turns into a woman and dances with the Prince. Following this dance, four of the smallest swans perform the *pas de quatre* (dance for four) which we hear on the recording.

As you listen, follow in your imagination the light, nimble movements and the bird-like turning of the dancers' heads. Here is the theme for this dance.

159

Goodbye, Old Paint

COWBOY SONG

This relaxed, easy-going cowboy song was used by Aaron Copland to help create a western atmosphere in the music for the ballet, "Billy the Kid."

Good - bye, Old Paint, I'm a - leav - in' Chey - enne. Good - bye, Old

Paint I'm a - leav - in' Chey - enne.
1. With my foot in the stir - rup, the
2. I'm a - rid - in' Old Paint, ___ and

reins in my hand. ___
lead - in' Old Sam. ___ } Good - bye, Old Paint, I'm a - leav - in' Chey - enne.

Billy the Kid

BY AARON COPLAND

"Billy the Kid" is a ballet. The story is told through dancing rather than the speaking voice, as in a play, or the singing voice, as in an opera. If we were to see the ballet, there would, of course, be no doubt in our minds as to what Aaron Copland's music is portraying at any given moment. However, the music itself is so dramatic that you will have little difficulty in following the story without seeing the dancers or stage sets. Below is a summary of the ballet's action.

The ballet opens with a march of the pioneers. Soon the scene changes to a frontier town and we see ranchers, cowboys, prospectors, dance-hall girls, and ranch women. A rodeo takes place, and the dancing becomes very vigorous. Just as Billy and his mother enter, a fight breaks out between two drunken cowboys. The fight becomes more and more violent, guns are drawn, and Billy's mother is accidentally killed by a stray bullet. Horror-stricken, Billy draws his knife and quickly stabs his mother's killer in the back, thus beginning his career as a killer and an outlaw.

In rapid succession, we see a series of episodes from Billy's later life. By the light of a campfire, Billy is seen playing cards with other outlaws. As dawn approaches, a posse appears led by Billy's former friend, Pat Garrett. The posse captures Billy and takes him off to jail, but Billy escapes and returns to hide in the desert with his sweetheart. He awakens from sleep, sensing that someone is coming. It is Pat Garrett and the posse. Receiving no answer to his question, "Who's there?" Billy lights a cigarette. The light of the match reveals his position in the dark and Pat Garrett shoots him. The scene changes to a group of mourning women and the ballet ends with the march of the pioneers.

The quiet, thinly-scored, "open" music sets the stage for the prairie scene. Then we hear the galloping horses (riding horses, lassoing, and fighting give this ballet, a vigorous, "manly" atmosphere), a Mexican dance, and the drunken fight clearly depicted. During the fight, the cowboy song, "Goodby, Old Paint" is heard for the first time (see opposite page). This song is used in many different ways throughout the ballet suite. The music becomes agitated as the fight worsens and it is not difficult to imagine when Billy stabs his mother's killer. We hear the quiet subdued night music when Billy is tracked down by the posse. After he is put in jail, the townspeople celebrate and we hear the music of a "drunken celebration." After Billy escapes to the lonely desert, we hear the lovely music which accompanies the *pas de deux* (dance for two people) with his sweetheart. Again, the music becomes threatening, the posse arrives—all is over.

161

Songs for Special Days

On pages 164 and 165, you will find an arrangement of "God Bless Our Land" for two trumpets and two trombones. This arrangement may be played to accompany the singing or as an independent instrumental selection.

God Bless Our Land

WORDS AND MUSIC
BY RICHARD KOUNTZ

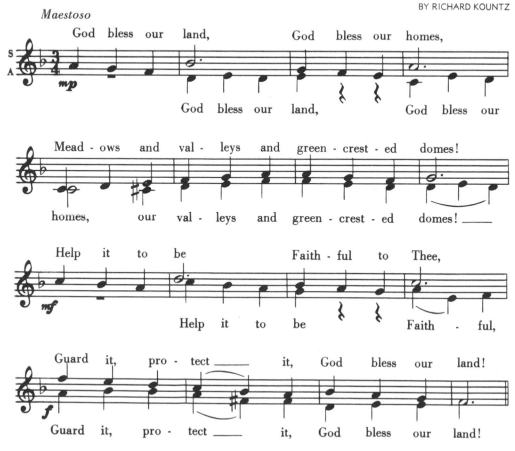

Maestoso

God bless our land, God bless our homes,

God bless our land, God bless our

Mead - ows and val - leys and green - crest - ed domes!

homes, our val - leys and green - crest - ed domes! ____

Help it to be Faith - ful to Thee,

Help it to be Faith - ful,

Guard it, pro - tect ____ it, God bless our land!

Guard it, pro - tect ____ it, God bless our land!

p Hm _____ Hm _____

MELODY

God bless our land, God guide its way,

Hm _____ Hm _____

Through doubt and per-il, from day un-to day!

mp Hm _____ Hm _____

mf

Its needs at-tend, Time with-out end;

MELODY

f Now and for-ev - er, God bless our land!

Now and for-ev - er, God bless our land!

163

God Bless Our Land

MUSIC BY RICHARD KOUNTZ

What does the brass quartet contribute to the mood of "God Bless Our Land"? Would the timbre of a woodwind or string quartet be equally appropriate?

164

The Star-Spangled Banner

WORDS BY FRANCIS SCOTT KEY

1. *Oh, say! can you see, by the dawn's early light,*
   What so proudly we hailed at the twilight's last gleaming?
   Whose broad stripes and bright stars, through the perilous fight,
   O'er the ramparts we watched were so gallantly streaming?
   And the rockets' red glare, the bombs bursting in air,
   Gave proof through the night that our flag was still there.
   Oh, say, does that Star-Spangled Banner yet wave
   O'er the land of the free and the home of the brave?

2. *On the shore, dimly seen through the mists of the deep,*
   Where the foe's haughty host in dread silence reposes,
   What is that which the breeze, o'er the towering steep,
   As it fitfully blows, half conceals, half discloses?
   Now it catches the gleam of the morning's first beam,
   In full glory reflected now shines on the stream;
   'Tis the Star-Spangled Banner, oh, long may it wave
   O'er the land of the free and the home of the brave!

3. *Oh, thus be it ever when free men shall stand*
   Between their loved homes and the war's desolation!
   Blest with vict'ry and peace, may the heav'n-rescued land
   Praise the Pow'r that hath made and preserved us a nation!
   Then conquer we must, when our cause it is just,
   And this be our motto: "In God is our trust."
   And the Star-Spangled Banner in triumph shall wave
   O'er the land of the free and the home of the brave!

We Plough the Fields

WORDS BY J. M. CAMPBELL
WELSH HYMN

How does the change from a minor I chord (G-Bb-D)
in the first ending to a major I chord (G-B-D)
in the second ending effect the mood?

Moderately

mf

1. We plough the fields and scat - ter the good seed on the land,
2. He on - ly is the mak - er of all things near and far,

But it is fed and wa - tered by God's al - might - y hand:
He paints the way - side flow - er, He lights the eve - ning star.

He sends the snow in win - ter, the warmth to swell the grain,
The wind and waves o - bey Him, by Him the birds are fed;

The breez - es and the sun - shine, the soft re - fresh - ing
Much more to us, His child - ren, He gives our dai - ly

DESCANT

mf   *f*

All ___ good gifts a - round ___ us are ___ sent from Heav'n a - bove,

MELODY

rain:
bread: *f* All good gifts a - round us are sent from Heav'n a - bove,

Then ___ thank the Lord, O ___ thank the Lord for all _____ His love. love.

Then thank the Lord, O thank the Lord for all His love. love.

O God, Beneath Thy Guiding Hand

MUSIC BY JOHN HATTON
WORDS BY THE REV. LEONARD BACON

Moderato

DESCANT

Ah

1. O God, be - neath Thy guid - ing hand
2. Laws, free - dom, truth, and faith in God
3. And here, Thy name, O God of love,

Ah

Our ex - iled fa - thers crossed the sea;
Came with those ex - iles o'er the waves;
Their chil - dren's chil - dren shall a - dore,

Ah

And when they trod the win - try strand,
And where their pil - grim feet have trod,
Till these e - ter - nal hills re - move,

Ah

With prayer and psalm they wor - shiped Thee.
The God they trust - ed guards their graves.
And spring a - dorns the earth no more.

O Hanukah

WORDS BY RUSSELL NORMAN
HEBREW FOLK MELODY
ADAPTED BY WALLACE SCHMIDT

Come, see the can - dles burn - ing, see them burn - ing so bright - ly;

The can - dles burn bright - ly; each

Can - dles burn - ing, burn - ing bright - ly;

See how each flame danc - es ev - er so light - ly.

flame danc - es light - ly.

See each flame dance, oh, so light - ly.

Ev - 'ry heart is gay when it's Ha - nu - kah time;

Ha - nu - kah, Ha - nu - kah, Ha - nu - kah, Ha - nu - kah,

What a hap - py

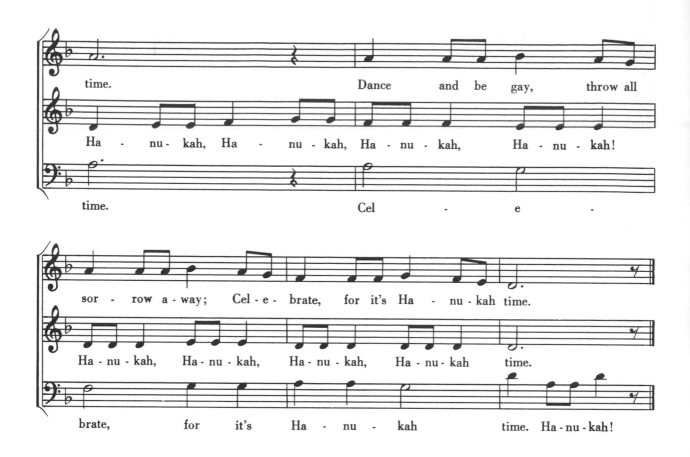

time. Dance and be gay, throw all

Ha - nu - kah, Ha - nu - kah, Ha - nu - kah, Ha - nu - kah!

time. Cel - e -

sor - row a - way; Cel - e - brate, for it's Ha - nu - kah time.

Ha - nu - kah, Ha - nu - kah, Ha - nu - kah, Ha - nu - kah time.

brate, for it's Ha - nu - kah time. Ha - nu - kah!

America, the Beautiful

WORDS BY KATHERINE LEE BATES

1. O beautiful for spacious skies,
   For amber waves of grain,
   For purple mountain majesties
   Above the fruited plain.
   America! America!
   God shed His grace on thee,
   And crown thy good with brotherhood
   From sea to shining sea!

2. O beautiful for pilgrim feet,
   Whose stern impassioned stress
   A thoroughfare for freedom beat
   Across the wilderness!
   America! America!
   God mend thine ev'ry flaw,
   Confirm thy soul in self-control,
   Thy liberty in law!

3. O beautiful for heroes proved
   In liberating strife,
   Who more than self their country loved,
   And mercy more than life!
   America! America!
   May God thy gold refine,
   Till all success be nobleness,
   And ev'ry gain divine!

4. O beautiful for patriot dream
   That sees, beyond the years,
   Thine alabaster cities gleam
   Undimmed by human tears!
   America! America!
   God shed His grace on thee,
   And crown thy good with brotherhood
   From sea to shining sea!

See the excerpt from the full band
score that appears on pages 138-139.

Stars and Stripes Forever

BY JOHN PHILIP SOUSA

The name John Philip Sousa makes us
think of marches and band music. The
fact that U.S.A. are the last letters of
Sousa's name is a happy coincidence, since
people all over the world associate his
marches with the spirit of America.

The melodies of this march, like all Sousa marches, are simple
but stirring. Here is the first of the three main melodies.

The first theme is repeated and the second theme is heard immediately. It, also,
is repeated and then we hear the famous
third theme. How many times is the third
theme repeated? What does Sousa do to
keep the repeats interesting?

171

Lullaby on Christmas Eve

Listen to the independent piano part.
Where does it imitate the voices?
In one word, how would you describe
the movement of the accompaniment?

TRANS. BY O. R. OVERBY
MUSIC BY F. M. CHRISTIANSEN

Quietly

1. Moth-er her vig-il is keep-ing, Hush, lit-tle babe, to her song; __
2. Moth-er in fer-vent de-vo-tion, Bends o'er thy cra-dle to-night, __

Rest thee se-cure in thy sleep-ing, Grow thee more state-ly and strong. __
Shields from all earth-ly com-mo-tion, Shel-ters her treas-ured de-light,

Slum-ber, slum-ber, Gen-tly thine eye-lids close;
Bid-ing, bid-ing, Car-ol-ing an-gels wait,

Slum - ber, slum - ber, Cra - dled in sweet re - pose. ____
Bid - ing. bid - ing, Vig - il at heav - en's gate. ____

O Come, All Ye Faithful

TRADITIONAL CAROL

Majestically

f
1. O come, all ye faith - ful, Joy - ful and tri - um - phant, O come ye,
2. Sing, choirs of An - gels, Sing in ex - ul - ta - tion, Sing, all
   A - des - te fi - de - les, Lae - ti tri - um - phan - tes, Ve - ni - te,

O come ____ ye to Beth - le - hem. Come and be - hold him, Born the King of
ye ci - ti - zens of Heav'n ____ a - bove: Glo - ry to God In the high - est,
Ve - ni - te in Beth - le - hem. Na - tum vi - de - te, Re - gem an - ge -

An - gels: O come, let us a - dore Him, O come, let us a - dore Him,
glo - ry! *Ve - ni - te, a - do - re - mus, Ve - ni - te, a - do - re - mus,*
lo - rum.

O come, let us a - dore Him, ____ Christ ____ the Lord.
Ve - ni - te, a - do - re - mus, ____ Do - mi - num.

173

A Mother's Lullaby

WORDS BY HENRY WINSTON
POLISH CAROL

Sing the upper voice part very softly. In the second verse, hum the upper part for a change of timbre and to heighten the peaceful mood.

Andante

Lull - a - by, Lull - a - by, Lull - a -

MELODY

mp 1. Lull - a - by, Je - sus, Oh, cease from your cry - ing, Here on Thy
2. See how the world lies in sor - row and sad - ness; Give all Thy

by, Lull - a - by.   MELODY

Moth - er's warm breast soft - ly ly - ing.   Lull - a - by, Je - sus, Oh,
bless - ing, Oh, bring Heav - en's glad - ness!

mp Lull - a - by, Lull - a - by.

MELODY

sleep now my treas - ure. Moth - er is watch - ing with love none can meas - ure.

From "The International Book of Christmas Carols"
© 1963 by Prentice-Hall, Inc.

What is typically Spanish in
the way the melody is harmonized
by the lower voice part?

Song of the Wise Men

TRANS. BY GEORGE K. EVANS
LATIN-AMERICAN CAROL

From a dis - tant land, The Sav - ior we come seek - ing,
De tie - rra le - ja - na Ve - ni - mos a ver - te,

Us - ing as our guide the star, so bright - ly beam - ing.
Nos sir - ve de gui - a La Es - trel - la de O - rien - te.

REFRAIN

Glo - ry in the High - est to the Son of Hea - ven,
Glo - ria en las al - tu - ras al Hi - jo de Di - os,

And up - on the earth be peace and love to men.
Glo - ria en las al - tu - ras y en la tie - rra a - mor.

Let It Snow!

WORDS BY SAMMY CAHN
MUSIC BY JULE STYNE

The refrain of "Let It Snow!" is in A-A-B-A form. Identify each section and find similarities and contrasts between the A and B sections.

Liltingly

mf The snow-man in the yard is fro-zen hard; He's a sor-ry sight to see.

If he had a brain, he'd com-plain; Bet he wish-es he were me.

REFRAIN

Oh! the weath-er out-side is fright-ful, But the fire is so de-light-ful,

And since we've no place to go, Let it snow! Let it snow! Let it snow!

It does-n't show signs of stop-ping, And I brought some corn for pop-ping;

The lights are turned 'way down low, Let it snow! Let it snow! Let it snow!

When we fi-nal-ly kiss good-night, How I'll hate go-ing out in the storm,

But if you'll real-ly hold me tight, All the way home I'll be warm.

The fire is slow-ly dy-ing, And, my dear, we're still good-bye-ing,

But as long as you love me so, Let it snow! Let it snow! Let it snow!

It Came Upon the Midnight Clear

TRADITIONAL CAROL

Andante

p

1. It came up-on ___ the mid-night clear, That glo - rious song ___ of old, ___
2. Still through the clo - ven skies they come, With peace - ful wings ___ un - furled; ___
3. For lo! the days ___ are has - t'ning on, By proph - ets seen ___ of old, ___

From an - gels bend - ing near the earth, To touch their harps ___ of gold: ___
And still their heav'n - ly mu - sic floats O'er all the wea - ry world: ___
When with the ev - er - cir - cling years Shall come the time fore-told, ___

mf

"Peace on the earth, ___ good will to men From heav'n's ___ all gra - cious King;" ___
A - bove its sad ___ and low - ly plains They bend ___ on hov - 'ring wing, ___
When the new heav'n ___ and earth shall own The Prince ___ of Peace ___ their King, ___

pp

The world in sol - emn still - ness lay To hear the an - gels sing. ___
And ev - er o'er ___ its Ba - bel sounds The bless - ed an - gels sing. ___
And the whole world ___ send back the song Which now the an - gels sing. ___

African Noel

ADAPTED FROM A LIBERIAN FOLK SONG
BY ADEN G. LEWIS

The form of this song is like an arch. It begins quietly, rises gradually to a vigorous climax, and gradually subsides to a quiet ending. Beginning with the music on the next page, you might add a clapping pattern on the offbeats. Follow the dynamics that appear in the drum part.

178

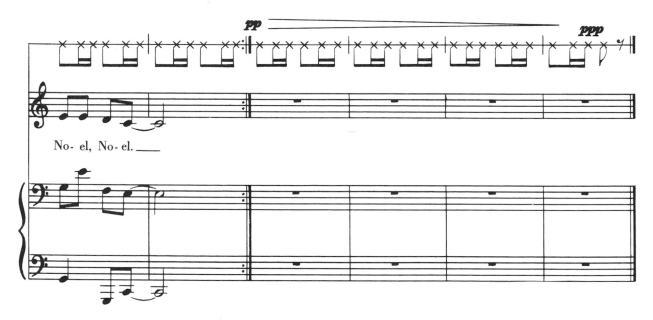

Yule, Yule

TRADITIONAL ROUND

You might sing or play one of the phrases of this round as an **ostinato.** Try to make up other seasonal verses that match the rhythm of the words.

Yule, Yule, The pud-ding's get-ting cool. Eat up, and cry, Yule!

Come, Hear the Wonderful Tidings

WORDS BY GEORGE K. EVANS
BOHEMIAN CAROL

1. Come, hear the wonderful tidings we bring: Bethlehem cradles a heavenly King! Come, sing His story, Come, sing His glory,

2. Mary, the sweet virgin mother so fine, Tenderly comforts the infant divine. Her face is glowing, with love o'er-flowing,

Je - sus____ is____ born!

For her____ dear____ Son.

Come,____ sing His sto - ry, Come,____ sing His glo - ry,

Her____ face is glow- ing, with____ love o'er- flow- ing,

3. Angels from heaven are singing His praise;
   Shepherds in wonder and joy on Him gaze;
   Bringing him honor, Presents they offer;
   Jesus, their Lord.

O Sons and Daughters

WORDS BY JEAN TISSERAND
16th CENTURY EASTER HYMN

1. O sons and daugh- ters, let____ us sing. The King of heav'n, the glor - ious King
2. How blest are they who have____ not seen And yet whose faith has con - stant been,
3. On this most ho - ly day____ of days Our hearts and voi - ces Lord,____ we raise

O'er death to- day____ rose tri - umph- ing. Hal - le- lu- jah, Hal- le- lu- jah!
For they e - ter - nal life____ shall win. Hal - le- lu- jah, Hal- le- lu- jah!
To Thee in ju - bi- lee____ and praise. Hal - le- lu- jah, Hal- le- lu- jah!

Musical Terms

A tempo — return to the original tempo
Accelerando — faster
Ritardando — slower
Crescendo (———————) — louder
Diminuendo (———————) — softer
Piano (**p**) — soft
Mezzo piano (**mp**) — medium soft
Pianissimo (**pp**) — very soft
Forte (**f**) — loud
Mezzo forte (**mf**) — medium loud
Fortissimo (**ff**) — very loud
Andante — at a walking pace
Allegro — lively
Moderato — moderately
Con spirito — with spirit
Staccato — detached
Da capo (D. C.) — repeat from the beginning
Dal segno (D. S.) — repeat from the sign

A meter signature consists of two numbers that appear on the staff following the key signature. The top figure indicates the number of beats in each measure, and the bottom figure refers to the duration of each beat. (Remember that tempo must also be considered in deciding upon the correct interpretation of a meter signature. For example, at a fast tempo, $\frac{6}{8}$ becomes $\frac{2}{?}$.)

Some meter signatures frequently used:

$\frac{2}{2}$ ¢ $\frac{2}{4}$ $\frac{3}{4}$ $\frac{4}{4}$ C $\frac{6}{8}$ $\frac{9}{8}$

NOTE VALUES		RESTS	
𝅝	Whole note	▬	Whole rest
𝅗𝅥	Half note	▬	Half rest
𝅘𝅥	Quarter note	𝄽	Quarter rest
𝅘𝅥𝅮	Eighth note	𝄾	Eighth rest
𝅘𝅥𝅯	Sixteenth note	𝄿	Sixteenth rest

 A staff provides a means of placing notes to indicate pitch.

 Treble or G clef locates the pitch G on the second line of the staff.

 Bass or F clef locates the pitch F on the fourth line of the staff.

A key signature consists of the sharps or flats (or absence of them) that appear on the staff following the clef sign.

♯   A sharp indicates the pitch of a note is raised one half-step.

♭   A flat indicates the pitch of a note is lowered one half-step.

♮   A natural cancels a sharp or flat.

>   An accent means a note is to be stressed.

⌒   A hold or *fermata* indicates that the note or rest is to be prolonged.

,   A breathing mark indicates a breath is to be taken.

//   A break mark signifies a complete pause.

𝅘𝅥.   A dot placed after a note increases the value of the note by one half.

 A tie is a curved line that increases the duration of the first note by the value of the note or notes to which it is tied.

 A slur is a curved line placed over or under two or more notes of different pitch to indicate that those notes are sung on one word or syllable.

 A light double bar indicates the end of a section, and a heavy double bar signifies the end of a composition.

 A repeat sign means a section is to be repeated. Either go back to the previous repeat sign; or if there is no previous repeat sign, go back to the beginning.

Circle of Keys

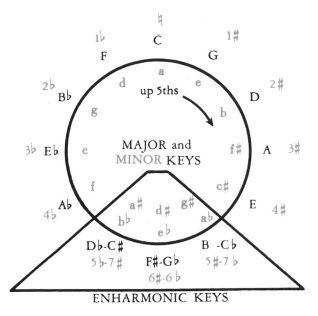

Great Staff and Keyboard

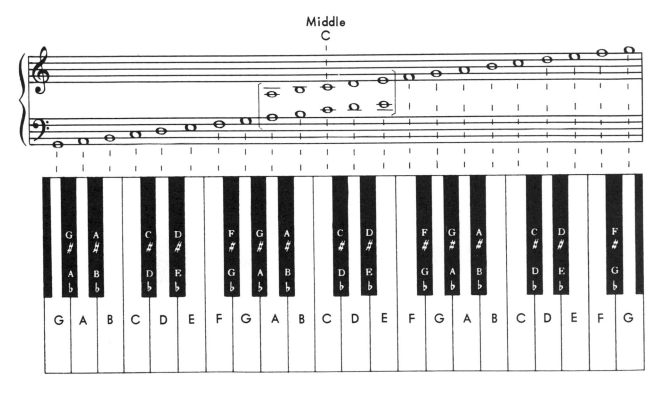

Classified Index

186

Song Titles

187

Listening Themes

Discussion Sections

Poems